Jo Seagar
BAKES

Jo Seagar
BAKES

PHOTOGRAPHY JAE FREW

RANDOM HOUSE
NEW ZEALAND

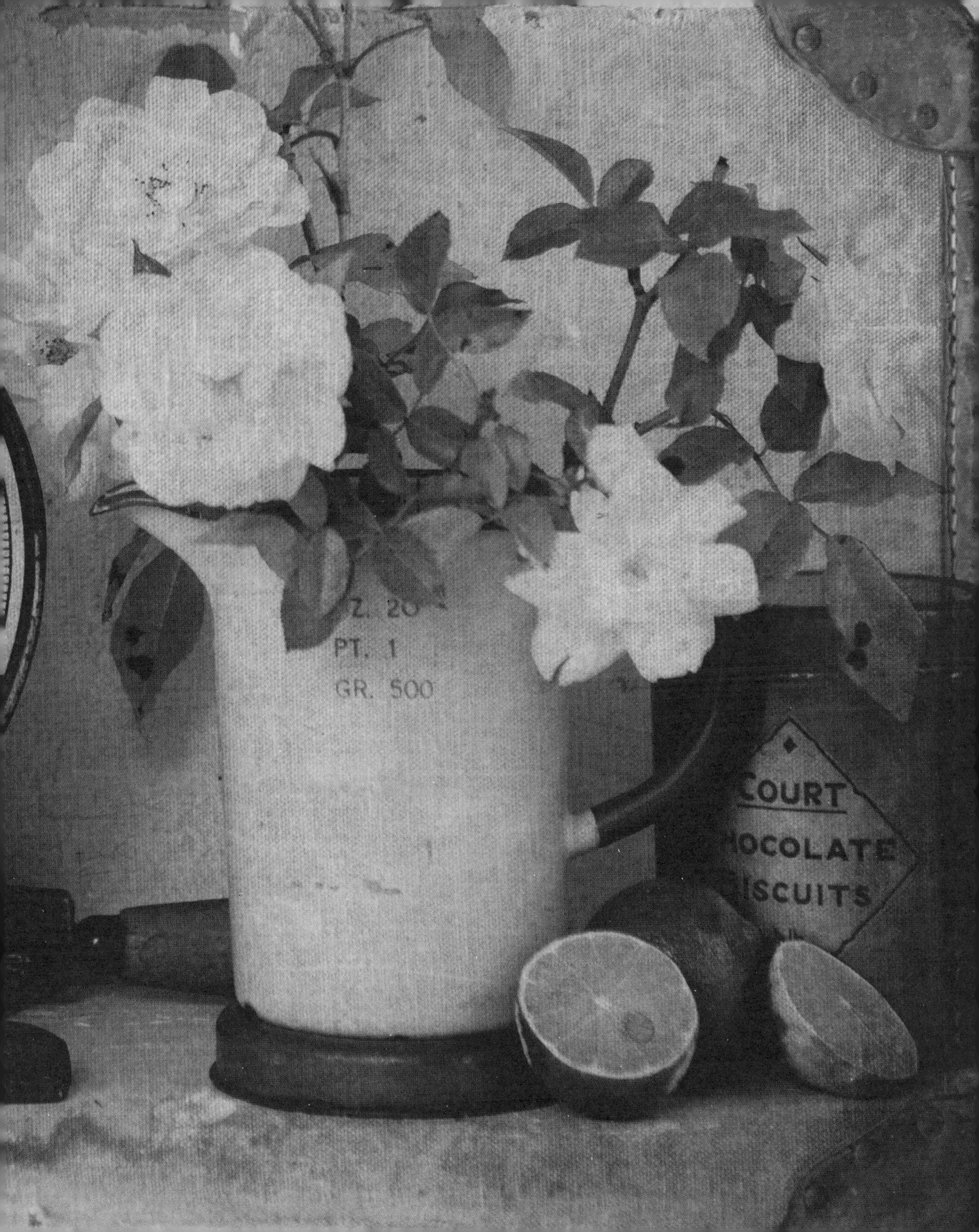
Z. 20
PT. 1
GR. 500
COURT
HOCOLATE
ISCUITS

A RANDOM HOUSE BOOK published by Random House New Zealand
18 Poland Road, Glenfield, Auckland, New Zealand

For more information about our titles go to www.randomhouse.co.nz
A catalogue record for this book is available from
the National Library of New Zealand

Random House New Zealand is part of the Random House Group
New York   London   Sydney   Auckland   Delhi   Johannesburg

First published 2014
© 2014 recipes and text Jo Seagar; photography Jae Frew

The moral rights of the author have been asserted
ISBN 978 1 77553 670 3

Design: Jae Frew and Petrina Jose
Cover photograph: Jae Frew

Printed in China by Everbest Printing Co Ltd

Dedication

I would like to dedicate this book to all those marvellously innovative cooks who have gone before me. The Mrs Buttons, Aunty Pegs and Granny Wins whose baking legacy and culinary presence lives on every time I rattle those pots and pans.

Jo Seagar

Contents

Start a family baking tradition today.

Introduction

Today, few people learn to cook at the side of their grandmother or mother, wearing a pinny and licking the wooden spoon like some Norman Rockwell or *Home Beautiful* poster.

The reality is that grannies often live miles away and mothers hold full-time jobs. Cooking's not an instinctive art, it's not in your DNA – no one is born an amazing cook. Like most things, it's learning and practice.

We travel, we taste, we are exposed to books and magazines and so much foodie television, and we are curious. Food and the smell of baking has the ability to bring back memories – some comforting recollection of freshly baked scones you arrived home to from school, or a birthday cake when you were five. Sometimes it's just fondly imagining how it used to be, or perhaps a yearning for a simple 'Waltons' family childhood. But the good news is you can learn to be a good cook.

I want to take the role of the teacher, reassuringly standing beside you, talking you through the stages of the recipe – demystifying the complicated jargon, explaining the important steps, and emphasising the major techniques and tips to ensure your personal success. I've done the faffing about, the testing and recipe development, so you just need to follow my lead and then stand by to receive the accolades and praise for the end result.

I've written this book to convey my passion for and pleasure in home baking, as well as explaining shortcuts, techniques and even tricky cheats that have taken me fifty-odd years to master. I want this to be your 'go to' baking book, full of delicious recipes that you can count on working successfully.

Baking is one area of cooking that has to be well thought out in advance. Unlike cooking a casserole or a stir-fry, you can't just make mid-course corrections. There is no way to add in the eggs when the cake is half baked! Of course there is plenty of room for artistic flourishes in the final icing, decorating and presentation of the results, but you do need to approach baking more like a scientist than an artist.

I don't have the desire or energy to bake things that are too fiddly, complicated or demanding, but I do love the praise baking brings. I admit I cook for the praise, and to me the effort required to bake something like a cake is so much less than the gratitude shown by the recipients. It's simple maths, and my kind of equation.

Happy cooking, everyone. Keep smiling. Keep baking.

Fondest love,

Jo Seagar

Anyone who is interested in baking is always interested in knowing more.

General Baking Info

COCOA

Chocolate always starts with cocoa pods, which are split open to reveal the coca beans inside. These are dried, roasted and refined into what we know as cocoa.

Cocoa can vary greatly. I generally use Dutch cocoa. This is nothing to do with Holland. 'Dutching' is the refining process used to make the cocoa and was developed by a Dutch chocolate-maker in the early 19th century. An alkali is used in the processing of Dutch cocoa, which removes some of the bitterness of the unrefined cocoa and neutralises its natural acidity.

CHOCOLATE

A good-quality chocolate can make all the difference in baking. Quality chocolate is measured by the quantity of cocoa solids.

To achieve good flavour a chocolate should have a cocoa-solids content of over 50% and preferably around 70%. Cheaper brands of chocolate may have had the cocoa content reduced and replaced with palm oil.

Couverture chocolate contains a high percentage of cocoa solids, no milk and no sugar.

Milk chocolate contains milk and usually sugar. Quality milk chocolate should still contain at least 30% cocoa solids.

Many generic brands of chocolate chips contain very little or no cocoa solids. Check the label, as chocolate with less cocoa and more palm oil will be harder to set, especially, for example, in ganache.

SUGAR

Caster sugar is a very fine complete sugar crystal. It is not just ground sugar. Caster sugar can't be made by whizzing sugar up in a food processor. Its unique crystal is sifted out of sugar, and good caster sugar should be very fine and uniform, very similar looking to salt.

We use caster sugar a lot in baking because its crystals dissolve quickly in liquids.

Brown sugar is white sugar combined with molasses. The darker the sugar the more molasses it contains. The molasses gives the sugar its rich flavour.

Tip: Place the crust from a slice of wholemeal bread in your brown sugar container. This will keep the sugar nice and soft.

BAKING POWDER & BAKING SODA (BICARBONATE OF SODA)

Both of these are rising or leavening agents that cause a batter to rise through a chemical reaction that produces carbon dioxide bubbles in the mixture.

They are not interchangeable as they react or do not react depending on the different ingredients in the recipe.

Baking soda produces its bubbly reaction when mixed with an acidic ingredient such as lemon juice, buttermilk or honey.

Baking powder produces its reaction when mixed with liquids.

General Baking Info (continued)

SELF-RAISING FLOUR

Self-raising flour is a flour mixed with a formulation of leavening agents. If you need to substitute baking powder and flour to produce self-raising flour, the nearest best formula is 2½ teaspoons of baking powder sifted and well mixed with 1 cup of flour. The result will always be better if you use prepared self-raising flour, if called for in a recipe, rather than mixing your own version.

BUTTERMILK

Some recipes call for buttermilk. If you do not have this, a good substitute can be made by combining 1½ teaspoons of cream of tartar with 1 cup of milk. This is a better substitute than adding vinegar or lemon juice to the milk.

CITRUS ZEST, RIND & PEEL

A citrus zester is a tool with little holes in it, which will produce longish thin curls of rind that are great for decorative uses.

For grated citrus rind I use a microplane grater. This produces a fine rind that's great for flavour and colour in cakes and icings. The microplane will also grate cheese such as parmesan, as well as fresh ginger and chocolate.

Using a vegetable peeler you can create long, thick curls of citrus peel. You need to be careful not to peel into the bitter white pith layer as well. Peeled rind is mainly used to infuse liquids and is generally strained out and discarded after use.

EGGS

When an egg is called for in my recipes it is a size seven egg, unless otherwise specified. It should be fresh, but sometimes an older egg is better for the recipe. For example, in meringues slightly older eggs result in thicker beaten egg whites with more volume. If you are using free-range eggs and you don't know what size they are, it is handy to remember that a size seven egg weighs 70 g in its shell. A size six weighs 60 g. A size seven egg has approximately 50 ml of egg white. Really big eggs often have two yolks.

MEASURING CUPS & SPOONS

In an ideal world everyone would measure ingredients using fine-tuned digital scales. However, I'm all about making baking easy and accessible, and I use cups and measuring spoons and a measuring jug for liquids. The important thing is to make sure your measuring cups are accurate. Check using a medicine measure from a chemist shop.

The whole world now uses a metric 250 ml measuring cup, 15 ml tablespoon and 5 ml teaspoon.

The only exception (no surprises) is Australia where they use a 20 ml tablespoon. Modern Australian food writers are more and more using the international standards, and you will now frequently see them write in recipes 1 tablespoon (15 ml), often with a note to Australian readers to beware.

You might think 5 ml (1 teaspoon) of something wouldn't make much of a difference, but try adding a teaspoon of cayenne pepper or chilli to a mixture and see the difference it makes. Lots of ingredients such as baking soda and cream of tartar are measured in small amounts. It is important to measure accurately.

A dessertspoon, teacup, large cup, heaped cup etc. are not acceptable measures in food writing.

To level off cups – I find using my finger perfectly acceptable, but do check the accuracy of your measuring spoons and cups. I have checked expensive porcelain cups that say they are 250 ml but are actually 380 ml, and a little cheap measuring jug that says 250 ml but is actually 190 ml. Price is not always an indicator of quality.

Metal measuring cups and spoons are best. Often a recipe requires you to warm the milk or golden syrup or to melt the butter. I use my metal measuring cups for this job as they are like mini saucepans. Check that yours are suitable to go on a gas, electric or induction element.

SILICONE SPATULAS

One of my first food memories is of licking the 'rubber scraper', a lovely old wooden-handled thing with swirly marbled rubber. Just the smell of them takes me back – and yes, you can still buy them, the rubber blade still falls off the wooden handle, and they still perish with age ...

I now use good-quality silicone spatulas that can withstand high temperatures. I prefer one with both a rounded side to scrape out rounded bowls and a flat side to scrape the sides of saucepans, and a flat-bottomed one to get into all the corners of a pan.

OVEN TEMPERATURES

Every oven is unique, even ones of the same make and model. The temperature dial is a fairly primitive instrument.

I use fan bake for all my baking, and all the temperatures in this book assume that fan bake is used. I suggest you use fan bake for everything. To me it means even temperatures.

The idea is that with the fan on you can technically bake four trays of biscuits evenly in the oven at the same time.

A simple, cheap oven thermometer will be your best friend. It will take all the guesswork out of knowing your oven's true temperature. Hang it from a shelf or sit it on the rack in the middle of your oven when preheating and find out what your oven temperature really is.

The temperature I have stated in each of these recipes is the real oven temperature with the fan bake function on.

CAKE TINS

Heavy, good-quality cake tins and baking trays are a good investment. They heat evenly and don't easily dent, bend or warp.

Spring-form tins are great for helping you remove delicate cakes gently from the tin. The best way to line the base of the spring-form tin is to cover the base with a sheet of baking paper, replace the rim of the tin and clip the side to fasten it, then cut away any excess paper. If the recipe requires you to line the sides, it is easy to cut a strip and simply trim to fit. Spraying the tin with baking spray before lining will ensure the paper sticks to the tin, not the cake.

In my cupboard I have:

- 20–21 cm round spring-form tin
- 23 cm round spring-form tin
- 25–26 cm round spring-form tin
- 20–21 cm square tin – can be spring-form
- 10 x 20 x 7 cm deep loaf tin
- 12 x 22 x 7 cm deep loaf tin
- 20 x 30 cm (standard) jelly roll, roulade or Swiss roll tin. A sheet of A4 paper sits neatly inside this.
- 25 x 35 cm Swiss roll tin. This is used for bigger slices and brownies.
- 12-cup Texas big muffin tin
- 12-cup standard muffin tin
- 24-cup mini-muffin tin
- a Bundt tin
- an Angel Food Cake tin
- a set of gem irons
- a set of patty pans
- a set of 24 small, flat-bottomed tart tins
- a Madeleine mould

SILICONE CAKE- & BAKEWARE

Silicone cake- and bakeware is becoming more readily available but I find it offers varying results. Some are so sticky that they almost glue the cake mixture to themselves. Really floppy cake pans and muffin trays are hard to use. You tend to place them on an oven tray to support the soft shape but this also works against the product – overheating the base and insulating it so the bottom of the baked goods either burn or sweat and don't colour or form a crisp crust, i.e. muffins.

Silicone moulds set into metal frames for muffins and mini-muffins work well. The metal distributes the heat evenly and they are self-supporting.

BAKING PAPER

This is a wonderful product, and I have standard width and wider commercial rolls in my cupboard. To avoid waste the paper can be wiped off and used again, particularly if it's used to line oven trays for biscuits.

Tip: If you have leftover whipped cream, use a piping bag to pipe rosettes onto a sheet of baking paper. Freeze, then keep frozen in a container in the freezer. These are great if you need to rush up a batch of pikelets or scones and want to serve them with whipped cream, or to float in hot chocolate.

WEIGHTS AND MEASURES

TEMPERATURE CONVERSIONS

DESCRIPTION	CELSIUS	FAHRENHEIT
Very low oven	150°C	300°F
Moderate oven	180°C	350°F
Hot oven	220°C	425°F
Very hot oven	230°C	450°F

LIQUID CONVERSIONS

5 ml	1 teaspoon
15 ml	1 tablespoon
250 ml	1 cup
600 ml	1 pint
1 litre	1¾ pints

NB: The Australian metric tablespoon measures 20 ml.

LENGTH CONVERSIONS

2.5 cm	1 inch
12 cm	4½ inches
20 cm	8 inches
24 cm	9½ inches
30 cm	12 inches

BISCUITS

Afghans are acknowledged as a New Zealand specialty biscuit. There is certainly nothing like them in Afghanistan. The name is possibly something to do with the shape of the biscuit, with the walnut on the top resembling a turban or hat worn in Afghanistan. They are my favourite biscuit.

AFGHANS

- 200 g butter
- ⅓ cup sugar
- 1 teaspoon vanilla
- 1 cup flour
- 2 tablespoons cocoa
- 1 teaspoon baking powder
- 1½ cups crushed cornflakes (lightly crush in your hands before measuring)

FOR THE ICING
- 1½ cups icing sugar
- 60 g butter
- 4 tablespoons boiling water
- ¼ cup cocoa
- walnut halves to decorate

Preheat the oven to 180°C. Line a baking tray with baking paper.

Beat the butter and sugar together until creamy, then add the vanilla. Mix in the flour, cocoa and baking powder, then stir in the crushed cornflakes. Place heaped teaspoonfuls of mixture onto the prepared tray and bake for 12–15 minutes. Cool on a wire rack before icing.

To make the icing, beat the icing sugar, butter, water and cocoa together until smooth and spread over the cooled biscuits. Top each with a walnut half. Store in an airtight container.

Prep time 10 minutes plus icing
Cook time 15 minutes

MAKES 20

GF

A delicious textured chewy biscuit which just happens to be gluten free, so that's a bonus. You can experiment with flavours by using grated lemon or lime rind or different flavoured honeys.

Chewy Almond, Honey & Orange Biscuits

➼ GLUTEN FREE

- ICING SUGAR, TO DUST (MAKE SURE THE ICING SUGAR IS GLUTEN FREE)
- 2 EGG WHITES
- 2 CUPS GROUND ALMONDS
- 1 CUP CASTER SUGAR
- GRATED RIND OF 1 ORANGE
- 1 TABLESPOON HONEY, WARMED

Preheat the oven to 160°C. Line 2 baking trays with baking paper. Place the icing sugar in a sieve and dust onto a large plate or into a shallow bowl.

Whisk the egg whites until soft peaks form, then add all the remaining ingredients and mix to a thick paste.

Break the mixture into small balls and roll in the icing sugar to coat well. Place on the prepared tray and gently press down, leaving plenty of room to spread.

(They just need to be pressed down slightly, not flattened out with a fork as you do with other biscuits.)

Bake for 15–18 minutes, then cool on a wire rack. Store for up to a week in an airtight container.

Prep time 10–15 minutes
Cook time 18 minutes

MAKES APPROX 24

There are loads of shortbread recipes and people get very fond of the one they are used to – a shortbread like their mother or grandmother made. A lovely old family friend, Thelma, gave me this recipe when I was 10 years old, about the time I first started collecting recipes in a notebook. She really stressed to me the importance of making three rows of fork holes in each biscuit – something I am quite fastidious about today. They just aren't the same without the fork indentations.

THELMA'S SHORTBREAD

- *250 g butter, softened to room temperature*
- *¾ cup icing sugar*
- *½ cup cornflour*
- *1½ cups flour*

Preheat the oven to 150°C. Line a baking tray with baking paper.

Beat the butter and icing sugar together until creamy. Mix in the cornflour and flour until well combined.

On a flour-dusted surface, roll out the dough to 1 cm thick and cut into fingers about 3 x 8 cm. Place these carefully on the prepared tray and prick each piece three times with a fork. Re-roll the scraps until you have used all the dough. Sometimes you end up with a funny little bit at the end, but this is known as the 'cook's tip'. You can eat that one as a check that they are all cooked properly.

Chill the tray for 15 minutes in the fridge or 5 minutes in the freezer.

Bake for 15–20 minutes, then lower the temperature to 130°C and cook a further 10 minutes. The biscuits shouldn't brown at all but be pale and golden and crisp. Cool a few minutes on the tray, then carefully remove to a wire rack to cool completely. Store in an airtight container for a week to 10 days.

Prep time 25 minutes
Chill time 15 minutes
Cook time 30 minutes

MAKES 26

Some recipes I've taken a few liberties with, while always paying my respects to the original versions.

This makes a large batch of biscuits to fill the tins for the week ahead. Great for school lunch boxes or after-school milk and cookies.

Oatmeal Raisin Biscuits

- 250 G BUTTER, SOFTENED TO ROOM TEMPERATURE
- 1 CUP SUGAR
- 1 CUP BROWN SUGAR
- 2 EGGS
- 2 TEASPOONS VANILLA
- 3 CUPS OATMEAL OR PORRIDGE OATS
- 2 CUPS FLOUR
- 1 TEASPOON BAKING SODA
- 1 TEASPOON SALT
- 1½ CUPS RAISINS OR SULTANAS

Preheat the oven to 180°C. Line 2 baking trays with baking paper.

Beat the butter and both sugars together until creamy and pale. Add the eggs and vanilla, then the oatmeal, flour, baking soda and salt. Mix well, then mix in the raisins.

Place heaped teaspoons of mixture onto the prepared trays, leaving room between for them to spread. Press flat with a wet fork.

Bake for 15–20 minutes until golden brown. Cool on the tray for 3 minutes, then carefully remove to a wire rack to cool completely.

Prep time 5 minutes
Cook time 20 minutes

MAKES 36

A quick and easy gluten-free recipe that gets top raves from all peanut butter lovers.

CRUNCHY PEANUT BUTTER BISCUITS

➤➤ GLUTEN FREE

- *2 cups crunchy peanut butter*
- *2 cups caster sugar*
- *2 eggs*

Preheat the oven to 170°C. Line a baking tray with baking paper.

Place all the ingredients in a bowl and mix well. Place teaspoonfuls of mixture onto the prepared tray, leaving room for spreading. Flatten each with a wet fork.

Bake for 15–20 minutes or until light golden brown. Cool on a wire rack and store in an airtight container for up to 10 days.

Prep time 2 minutes
Cook time 20 minutes

MAKES 24

This New Zealand-style old-fashioned coconut macaroon has an almond on top. This was my job as a little girl – placing the almonds 'just so' on the biscuits before they went into the oven.

GRANNY'S COCONUT MACAROONS

- *3 egg whites, at room temperature*
- *¼ teaspoon salt*
- *1 cup caster sugar*
- *½ teaspoon vanilla or almond essence*
- *2 tablespoons flour*
- *1½ cups coconut*
- *36 blanched almonds*

Preheat the oven to 150°C. Line 2 baking trays with baking paper.

Beat the egg whites with the salt until they form peaks which turn over, then add half the sugar and beat until the peaks stand upright when the beater is removed from the mixture. Stir in the vanilla or almond essence.

Mix together the remaining sugar with the flour and coconut, and then fold into the egg white mixture.

Evenly spoon out the mixture into little rounds on the prepared trays. Press a whole blanched almond into the top of each biscuit.

Bake for 20–25 minutes. The biscuits should feel quite firm on the outside, but be chewy inside. Cool on a wire rack and store in an airtight container for up to 10 days.

Prep time 15 minutes
Cook time 25 minutes

MAKES 36

THESE ARE OFTEN CALLED LAVA
OR CRINKLE COOKIES AND HAVE
A DISTINCTIVE SOFT CRUST AND
CHEWY CENTRE.

Chocolate Spiced Crinkle Cookies

- 1¼ CUPS FLOUR
- ½ CUP COCOA
- 2 TEASPOONS MIXED SPICE
- 1 TEASPOON BAKING POWDER
- 1 CUP CASTER SUGAR
- 60 G BUTTER, CHILLED & CHOPPED FINELY INTO SMALL CUBES OR GRATED
- 2 EGGS
- 1 TEASPOON VANILLA
- 1 CUP ICING SUGAR

Place the flour, cocoa, mixed spice, baking powder and caster sugar in the bowl of an electric mixer. Run the machine as you add the little cubes or grated butter. Mix until the butter is well distributed. Add the eggs and vanilla and mix well. Chill in the bowl in the refrigerator for an hour.

Preheat the oven to 200°C. Line 2 baking trays with baking paper.

Place the icing sugar in a small bowl. Sift if it is lumpy.

Roll the dough into small walnut-sized balls and toss in icing sugar to coat them well.

Place on the prepared trays about 5–6 cm apart to allow them to expand. Resist the urge to squash them flat; just leave as small balls, which will spread and deflate as they cook.

Bake for 12–14 minutes. They should be just set. Cool on the tray for 5 minutes, then transfer to a wire rack to cool completely. Store in an airtight container for up to a week.

Prep time 5 minutes
Chill time 1 hour
Cook time 15 minutes

MAKES 30

These classic Kiwi biscuits were a part of my New Zealand childhood. I remember making them as a small girl, helping my mother in the weekends filling the tins in anticipation of the busy week ahead.

HOKEY POKEY BISCUITS

- *125 g butter*
- *½ cup sugar*
- *1 tablespoon milk*
- *1 tablespoon golden syrup*
- *1 teaspoon baking soda*
- *1½ cups flour*

Preheat the oven to 180°C. Line a baking tray with baking paper.

Beat the butter and sugar together until pale and creamy. Warm the milk and golden syrup in a small saucepan or microwave jug. Add the baking soda and mix well. Mix all the ingredients together until well combined.

Roll into small balls. Place on the prepared tray and flatten with a wet fork. Bake for 15–20 minutes until golden. Cool on a wire rack.

Prep time 6 minutes
Cook time 20 minutes

MAKES APPROX 36 SMALL OR 24 LARGE COOKIES

A family recipe from my childhood when we lived at 'Claremont' farm in Hawke's Bay. A great biscuit for gifts – those 'hard to buy for' people love a homemade bickie. These are quick and easy and the recipe makes a decent big batch – we always have these in the biscuit tins over the holidays.

Claremont Spice Biscuits

- 250 G BUTTER
- 1½ CUPS SUGAR
- 1 EGG
- 1 TABLESPOON GOLDEN SYRUP
- 2 CUPS FLOUR
- 1 TEASPOON BAKING POWDER
- 2 TEASPOONS MIXED SPICE

Preheat the oven to 180°C. Line 2 baking trays with baking paper.

Beat the butter and sugar together until creamy, add the egg and golden syrup, then mix in the dry ingredients.

Roll teaspoonfuls of mixture into little balls and place on the prepared trays. Flatten with a wet fork.

Bake for 12–15 minutes until golden brown. Cool on a wire rack. Store in an airtight container for up to 10 days.

Prep time 5 minutes
Cook time 15 minutes

MAKES APPROX 36

Gorgeous with coffee, these delicious treats are easy to make and are always delightfully received if made as a gift.

FLORENTINES

➵ GLUTEN FREE

- 3 cups cornflakes (lightly crushed in your hand before measuring)
- ¾ cup flaked almonds
- ½ cup dried cranberries
- 12–15 glacé cherries, thinly sliced
- 1 x 400 g can sweetened condensed milk
- 1 x 375 g packet chocolate melts (milk, white or dark chocolate; check that it is GF chocolate)

Preheat the oven to 180°C. Line 2 baking trays with baking paper.

Mix the cornflakes, almonds, cranberries and cherries in a large bowl. Mix in the condensed milk. The mixture will be really gluggy and sticky.

Spoon tablespoons of the mixture onto the prepared trays, leaving room between for them to spread. Flatten with the back of a wet spoon.

Bake for 8–10 minutes until golden. Cool on the trays for 5 minutes, then carefully slide off and turn upside down on a wire rack to cool completely.

Melt the chocolate following the packet instructions. Brush the bases of the florentines with a generous layer of melted chocolate and allow to set. Some people like to use the prongs of a fork to make squiggly patterns in the chocolate. This makes them look more traditional. Keep for up to a week in an airtight container.

Prep time 5 minutes plus icing
Cook time 10 minutes

MAKES 24

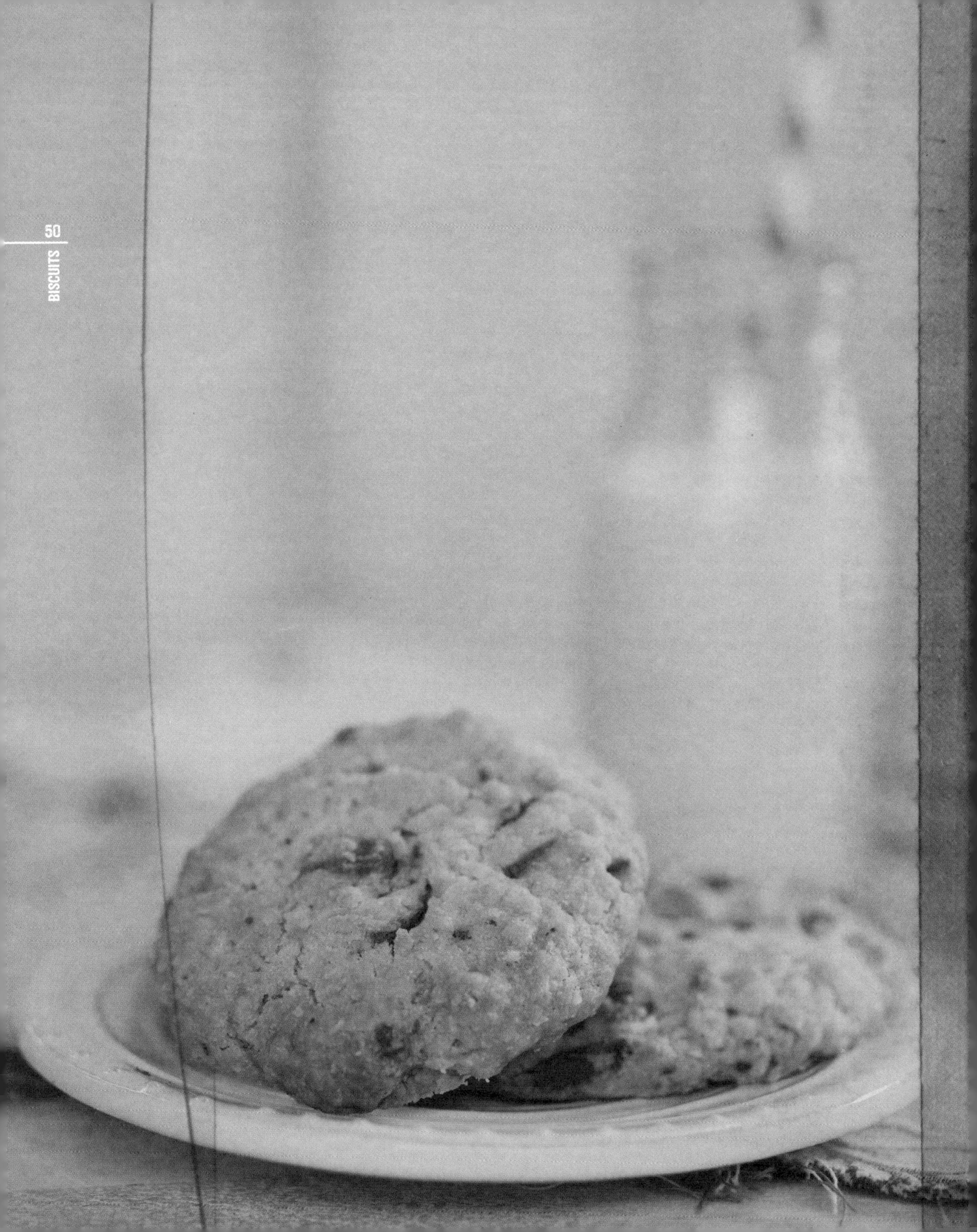

These are my family's absolute favourite. I've been making them for years and it's probably my most frequently requested recipe. I think they are made by cooks all around the country these days. They are very good. They won't sit around for long, but will keep in an airtight container for up to 10 days.

Chocolate Chunk Oat Cookies

- 250 G BUTTER, SOFTENED
- 3 TABLESPOONS SWEETENED CONDENSED MILK
- ¾ CUP SUGAR
- 1½ CUPS FLOUR
- 1½ CUPS ROLLED OATS (I USE WHOLEGRAIN ONES, WHICH AREN'T SO FLATTENED AND PORRIDGE-LIKE)
- 1 TEASPOON BAKING POWDER
- 200 G CHOCOLATE, ROUGHLY CHOPPED (LIGHT OR DARK OR WHITE CHOCOLATE)

Preheat the oven to 170°C. Line 2 baking trays with baking paper.

Beat the butter, condensed milk and sugar together until light and very pale and creamy. Add the flour, rolled oats, baking powder and chocolate chunks and mix well. Place tablespoonfuls of the mixture onto the prepared trays. Press down with a wet fork.

Cook for 18–20 minutes until golden brown. Cool on a wire rack and store in an airtight container for up to 10 days.

You can vary this recipe very simply – substitute dried fruit for the chocolate; substitute nuts; use a mixture of dark milk and white chocolate, or use fruit and nut chocolate.

Prep time 10 minutes
Cook time 20 minutes

MAKES 24-30

A Seagar family favourite biscuit. A big vanilla taste in a pale, nutty cookie – like a blonde version of a peanut brownie.

SALTED ROAST PEANUT BLONDIE BISCUITS

- 300 G BUTTER
- 1 CUP SUGAR
- 2 TEASPOONS VANILLA
- 2 CUPS SELF-RAISING FLOUR
- 2 CUPS SALTED ROASTED PEANUTS

Preheat the oven to 180°C. Line 2 baking trays with baking paper.

In a bowl, beat together the butter and sugar until creamy. Add the vanilla, flour and peanuts. Place teaspoonfuls of the mixture onto the prepared trays, leaving room to spread between each.

Bake for 15–18 minutes. Allow to cool a few minutes on the tray before removing to a wire rack. Store in an airtight container.

Prep time 5 minutes
Cook time 18 minutes

MAKES 30-36

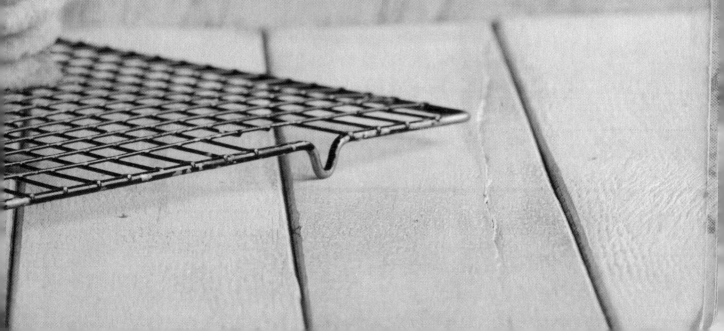

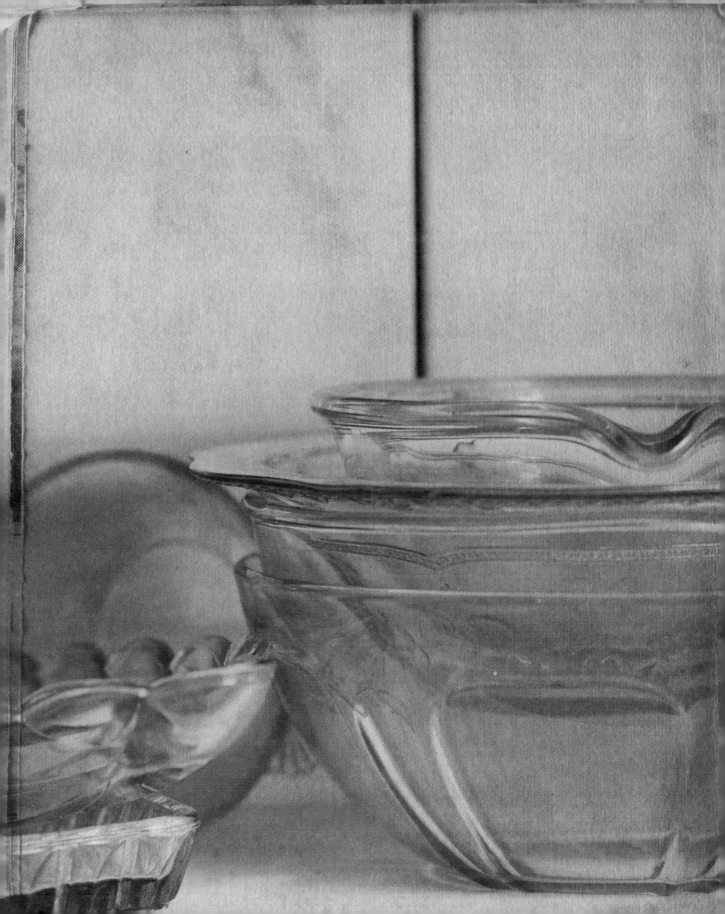

My friend Betty gave me her special Spicy Gingernut recipe. It's a recipe she had been making for years, and I always think of her as I run up a batch of these addictive, delicious, crisp biscuits. Perfect for dunking.

Betty's Spicy Gingernuts

- 100 G BUTTER, SOFTENED
- 1 CUP CASTER SUGAR
- 1 TABLESPOON GOLDEN SYRUP
- 1 EGG
- 1⅓ CUPS FLOUR
- 1 TEASPOON BAKING POWDER
- 2 TEASPOONS CINNAMON
- 1 TABLESPOON GROUND GINGER

Preheat the oven to 180°C. Line 2 baking trays with baking paper.

Beat the butter, caster sugar and golden syrup together until really fluffy and light. Add the egg and beat well, then add the dry ingredients and mix well.

Roll into 30 small walnut-sized balls and place on the trays. DO NOT FLATTEN.

Bake for 15–18 minutes. Cool on a wire rack, then store in an airtight container for up to 10 days.

Prep time 10 minutes
Cook time 18 minutes

MAKES 30

These were originally known as German biscuits, the recipe no doubt brought to New Zealand by German settlers. After World World 1 they discreetly changed their name to Belgium Biscuits as anti-German feelings ran high.

BELGIUM BISCUITS

- 125 g butter
- ¼ cup brown sugar
- 1 egg
- 1 teaspoon cinnamon
- 2 teaspoons mixed spice
- 2 cups flour
- 1 teaspoon cocoa
- 1 teaspoon baking powder

FOR THE FILLING & ICING

- 1 cup icing sugar
- ½ teaspoon raspberry essence
- a few drops pink food colouring
- boiling water to mix
- 1 packet raspberry jelly crystals
- ¾ cup raspberry jam

Preheat the oven to 180°C. Line 2 baking trays with baking paper.

Beat the butter and brown sugar together until smooth and light-coloured. Add the egg and spices and mix to combine. Mix in the flour, cocoa and baking powder.

Turn the dough out onto a floured board and gently roll to a thickness of 3–4 mm. Using a 4–5 cm cookie cutter, press out rounds of dough and place on the prepared trays, leaving enough room for them to spread a little. Re-roll the scraps until you have used all the dough. Chill the trays for 15 minutes in the fridge before cooking.

Bake for approximately 15–18 minutes – remove from the oven as soon as the edges begin to brown. Cool on a wire rack.

Mix the icing sugar, raspberry essence and food colouring with enough boiling water to create a spreadable icing.

When the biscuits are completely cool, ice half of the biscuits with the pink icing then sprinkle raspberry crystals over the wet icing so that they stick well to the surface. Spread the other half of the biscuits with raspberry jam. When the icing is set, sandwich the iced and jammed biscuits together. Store in an airtight container for up to a week.

Prep time 10 minutes plus icing
Chill time 15 minutes
Cook time 18 minutes

MAKES APPROX 20 ICED & SANDWICHED-TOGETHER BISCUITS

These are the most famous of New Zealand's own biscuits, named after the Australian & New Zealand Army Corps soldiers who fought at Gallipoli in World War 1. There are some family histories stating these biscuits were sealed in tins and sent to the army boys in the battlefield due to their long-keeping ability.

Classic Anzac Biscuits

- 125 G BUTTER
- 2 TABLESPOONS COLD WATER
- 2 TABLESPOONS GOLDEN SYRUP
- 1 TEASPOON BAKING SODA
- 1 CUP ROLLED OATS
- 1 CUP COARSE THREAD COCONUT
- 1 CUP FLOUR
- 1 CUP BROWN SUGAR

Preheat the oven to 160°C. Line 2 baking trays with baking paper.

In a medium to large saucepan place the butter, cold water and golden syrup. Place over medium heat and melt the butter, bringing almost to the boil. Add the baking soda and remove from the heat. Mix in the dry ingredients and combine well. Roll the mixture into small balls, the size of a large walnut. Press flat onto the prepared trays, allowing a little room between each for the biscuits to spread.

Bake for 15–18 minutes. Cool on the tray for 5 minutes before transferring to a wire rack to cool completely. Store in an airtight container for up to a month.

Note: I've actually tested four- and five-month-old biscuits and they are just fine and still crisp, so long as they are stored in an airtight container.

Prep time 10 minutes
Cook time 18 minutes

MAKES 26-28

FARMHOUSE COCONUT CRISPIES

➤ GLUTEN & DAIRY FREE

- ½ cup caster sugar
- 2 eggs, separated
- 1 cup coconut
- ½ teaspoon coconut essence

Preheat the oven to 150°C. Line 2 baking trays with baking paper.

Beat the sugar and egg yolks together until pale and thick. Mix in the coconut and essence. In a separate bowl, beat the egg whites until stiff and then fold into the coconut mixture.

Place teaspoonfuls of mixture on the trays, leaving room around each as they spread out. The mixture is quite runny.

Bake for 15 minutes, then reduce the heat to 110°C and bake a further 15 minutes. Cool on a wire rack and store in an airtight container.

Prep time 10 minutes
Cook time 30 minutes

MAKES 36-40

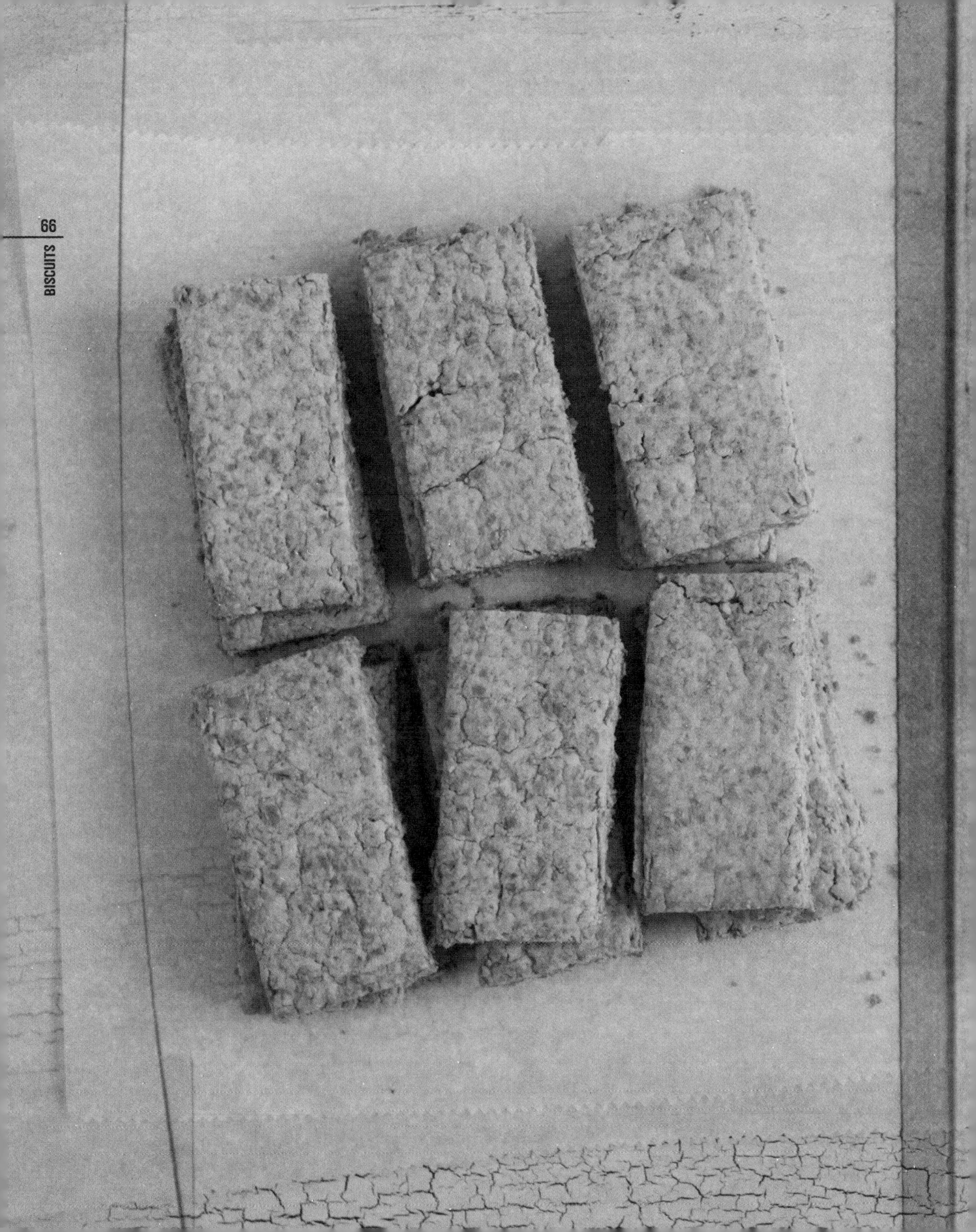

Delicious buttered and eaten with a cup of tea or served with cheese on a cheeseboard – particularly good with blue cheese.

Bran Biscuits

- 100 G BUTTER, SOFTENED TO ROOM TEMPERATURE
- 2 TABLESPOONS SUGAR
- 1 EGG
- 1½ CUPS BRAN FLAKES
- 1 CUP SELF-RAISING FLOUR
- ½ CUP WHOLEMEAL FLOUR
- ½ TEASPOON SALT

Preheat the oven to 180°C. Line 2 baking trays with baking paper.

Beat the butter and sugar together until pale and light. Add the egg and beat well. Mix in the bran, flours and salt and combine well.

Dust a surface with flour and roll out the mixture to 4–5 mm thick. Cut into fingers 3 x 7 cm and place on the tray, leaving room between to spread.

Bake for 15–18 minutes until firm and lightly golden. Cool on a wire rack and store in an airtight container for up to 2 weeks.

Prep time 10 minutes
Cook time 18 minutes

MAKES APPROX 24–26

These are melt-in-the-mouth biscuits and very popular for an afternoon tea treat. We make loads of them for our café every day.

YO-YOS

- *180 g butter, softened to room temperature*
- *¾ cup icing sugar*
- *1 teaspoon vanilla*
- *½ cup custard powder*
- *1 teaspoon baking powder*
- *1½ cups flour*

Preheat the oven to 160°C. Line 2 baking trays with baking paper.

Place all the the ingredients in the bowl of a cake mixer and mix until well combined. With floured hands, roll the mixture into small balls. If the mixture is too soft, cool for 10 minutes in the fridge, then try again. Place the balls on the prepared trays and press down, but not too flat, with a wet fork.

Bake for 18–20 minutes until very lightly golden and quite firm, but not browned.

Cool on a wire rack.

When cold, join two biscuits together with lemon butter icing. This can be piped or spread on the biscuits. Store in an airtight container for up to a week.

Prep time 10 minutes
Cook time 20 minutes plus assembly

MAKES ABOUT 15 SANDWICHED-TOGETHER BISCUITS

LEMON BUTTER ICING

- *2 tablespoons lemon juice*
- *1 tablespoon butter*
- *1 teaspoon grated lemon rind*
- *2 cups icing sugar*
- *1 tablespoon custard powder*

Heat the lemon juice and butter together until the butter has melted. Mix in the lemon rind, icing sugar and custard powder.

Beat until a thick, smooth icing consistency.

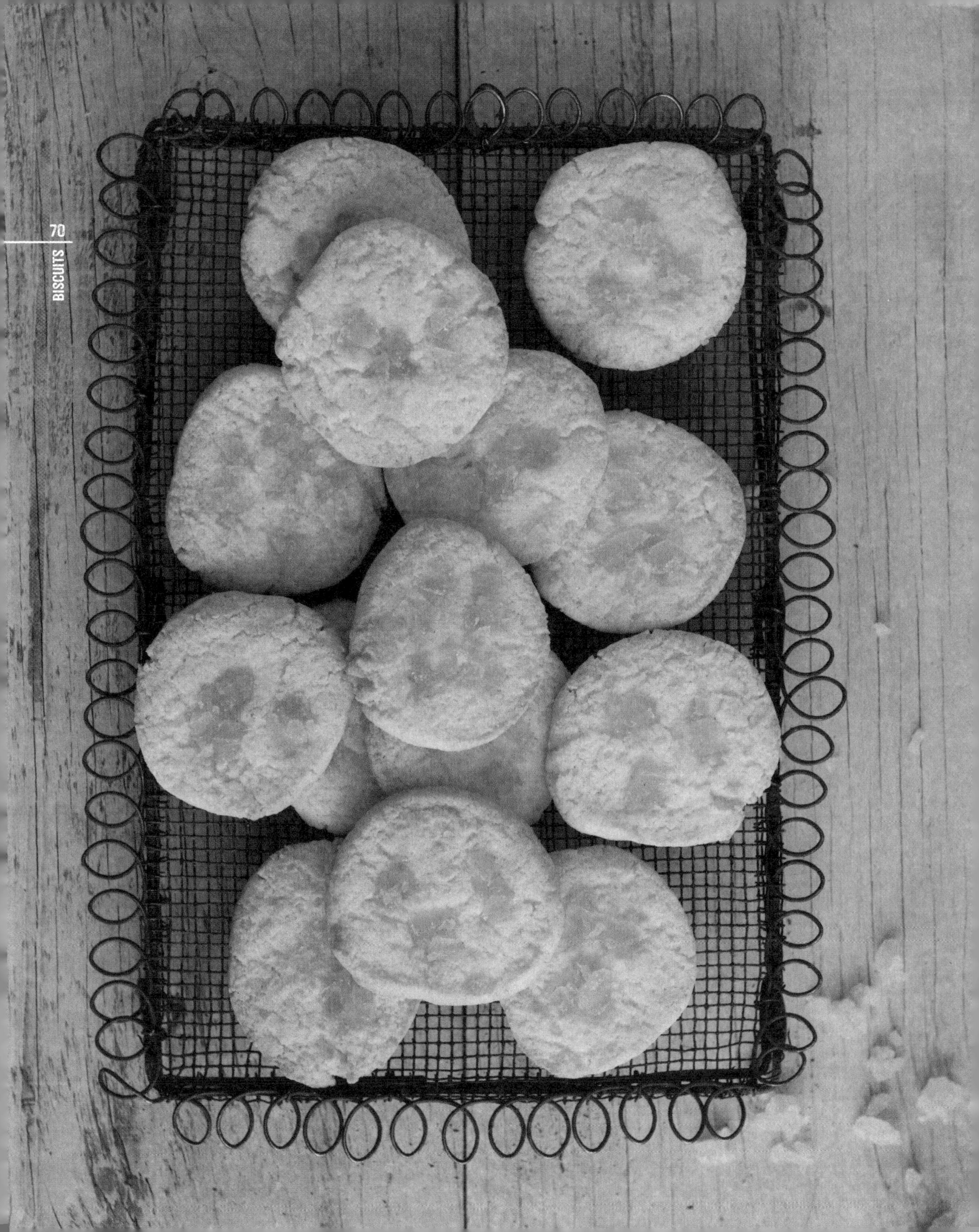

Ginger Crispy Cracknels

- 1 CUP FLOUR
- 1 TEASPOON BAKING POWDER
- 60 G BUTTER
- 1 CUP WHITE SUGAR
- 1 CUP MEDIUM-CUT COCONUT
- 1 EGG
- ½ CUP FINELY CHOPPED CRYSTALLISED GINGER
  FOR TOPPING

Preheat the oven to 160°C. Line 2 baking trays with baking paper.

Place the flour, baking powder, butter and sugar in a food processor and run the machine to mix well. Add the coconut and pulse to just mix through. Break the egg into the food processor and run the machine until the dough clumps together around the blade.

With floured hands, roll the dough into a sausage-shaped log, approximately 4–5 cm in diameter, and slice into little rounds half a centimetre thick.

Place on the prepared trays. Place a half-teaspoon of chopped ginger on the top of each biscuit and press in lightly. Bake for 10–12 minutes.

The biscuits tend to puff up then sink when they come out of the oven. Rest for 2 minutes on the tray before removing to cool thoroughly (and crisp up) on a wire rack. Store in an airtight container for 10–14 days.

Prep time 20 minutes
Cook time 12 minutes

MAKES 28-30

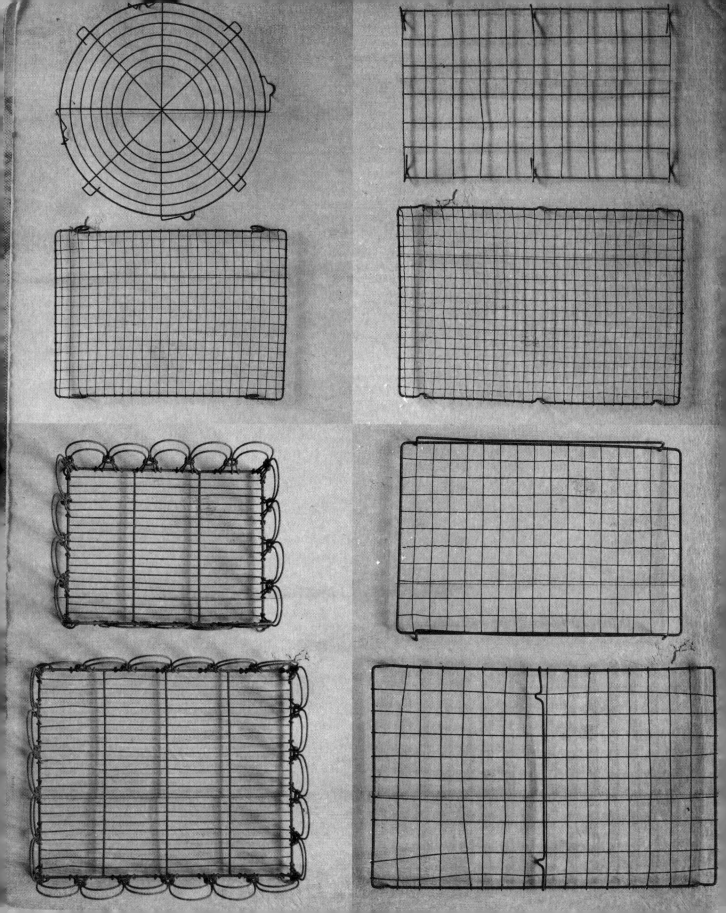

Freeze a few unbaked
biscuits to have at the
ready for when you
need fresh baking fast.

These are an old English or maybe even Welsh traditional Easter biscuit. They are so simple to make and quite delicious, you'll be like me and make them all the time, not just at Easter. For my family, they are as much a part of Easter as Hot Cross Buns and Easter eggs.

EASTER SUGAR CRUST BISCUITS

- *175 g butter, softened to room temperature*
- *¾ cup caster sugar*
- *grated rind of 1 lemon*
- *2 eggs, separated*
- *2 cups flour*
- *½ cup currants*
- *½ cup sugar for dredging*

Preheat the oven to 160°C. Line 2 baking trays with baking paper.

Beat the butter and sugar together until pale and creamy. Add the lemon rind and egg yolks, then quickly mix in the flour and currants. Roll teaspoonfuls of mixture into small balls, about the size of a walnut, and press flat with a wet fingertip.

Whisk the egg whites until frothy (not stiffly beaten). Place the extra sugar on a saucer.

Dunk or brush the flattened biscuits with egg white, then dredge with sugar and place on the prepared trays.

Bake for 18–20 minutes until pale golden. Cool on a wire rack and store in an airtight container or tightly sealed in cellophane bags for gift giving.

Prep time 15 minutes
Cook time 20 minutes

MAKES 20-24

In my mother's family recipe books these are known as Cheese Biscuits For Bridge Parties. They are best served warm and are like a savoury shortbread.

Cheese Biscuits

- 150 G BUTTER
- 150 G (ABOUT 1½ CUPS) GRATED TASTY CHEESE
- 1½ CUPS FLOUR
- SALT & PEPPER TO TASTE

Options for toppings
- FINELY GRATED CHEESE
- CRUSHED POTATO OR CORN CHIPS
- SESAME OR POPPY SEEDS
- CRUSHED CARDAMOM
- LEMON PEPPER SEASONING
- CAJUN SPICE MIX
- SEA SALT FLAKES OR COARSELY GROUND ROCK SALT
- CELERY OR FENNEL SEEDS
- FINELY GRATED PARMESAN CHEESE

Place the butter, cheese, flour, and salt and pepper in a food processor and run the machine until the pastry clings in a lump around the blade.

With floured hands remove the mixture and form into sausage-shaped logs. Wrap in cling film and chill for 20 minutes.

Preheat the oven to 180°C. Line 2 oven trays with baking paper.

Slice each log into 3–4 mm thick rounds. Spread out on the prepared trays, pressing any optional extra bits and pieces into the surface (sesame seeds or crushed potato chips or any of the options above). Bake for 15–20 minutes until golden brown.

Cool the biscuits for 2–3 minutes on the trays before sliding them carefully off onto a wire rack to cool completely. Store in an airtight container.

Prep time 3 minutes
Chill time 20 minutes
Cook time 20 minutes

MAKES 26

These make wonderful presents such as a 'thank you to the teacher' type gift. Easy to make and always greatly appreciated by the recipient.

SPECIAL CHRISTMAS COOKIES

- *125 g butter*
- *1 cup sugar*
- *1 egg*
- *1 teaspoon vanilla*
- *1 teaspoon mixed spice*
- *1¼ cups flour*
- *½ teaspoon baking soda*
- *½ teaspoon salt*
- *1 cup chopped nuts (walnuts, pecans, etc.)*
- *1 cup chocolate chips or chopped dark chocolate*
- *1 cup coarse thread coconut*
- *1 cup mixed red & green glacé cherries, each chopped into 2–3 pieces*

Preheat the oven to 170°C. Line 2 oven trays with baking paper.

Beat the butter and sugar together until creamy. Mix in the egg and vanilla, then the remaining ingredients.

Put teaspoonfuls of the mixture onto the prepared trays, not too closely together as they will spread out a little, and flatten with a wet fork. Bake for 15 minutes.

Cool on a wire rack. Store in an airtight container or sealed in cellophane for gift giving.

Note: These can be half dipped or drizzled with melted chocolate as an extra treat.

Prep time 10 minutes
Cook time 15 minutes

MAKES 24–28

I often make these in a food processor as it chops up the oat bran or rolled oats into a more finely ground product, resulting in a smoother-textured oatcake. Perfect to accompany blue cheese or traditional crumbly cheddar.

Scottish Oatcake Digestive Biscuits

- 200 G BUTTER, SOFTENED
- ½ CUP BROWN SUGAR
- 1 EGG
- ¾ CUP FLOUR
- ½ TEASPOON BAKING SODA
- 2¼ CUPS OAT BRAN OR ROLLED OATS
- ½ TEASPOON SALT

Preheat the oven to 180°C. Line an oven tray with baking paper.

Beat the butter and brown sugar together until creamy. Beat in the egg, then add the remaining ingredients. Mix well. Shape the mixture into a round block and wrap in cling film. Chill in the fridge for 30 minutes.

Roll out on a floured surface to 4–5 mm thick and press out 5–6 cm rounds with a cookie cutter (or a glass). Place on the prepared tray, allowing a little room between each for expansion while cooking.

Bake for 15–20 minutes until light honey golden. Cool on a wire rack and store in an airtight container for up to 2 weeks. They freeze well but require a re-warm in the oven to freshen them up to a just-baked product.

Prep time 5 minutes
Chill time 30 minutes
Cook time 20 minutes

MAKES 30-40

These can be made into Gingerbread Men or Christmas cookies, or cut-out animals, jet planes, dinosaurs or Easter egg shapes. A very user-friendly and versatile gingerbread dough. Perfect to decorate with icing.

GINGERBREAD COOKIES

- 250 g butter, softened
- 1 cup icing sugar
- 2 eggs
- ½ cup golden syrup, warmed
- 4 cups flour
- 1 tablespoon cocoa
- 1 tablespoon ground ginger
- 2 teaspoons mixed spice
- 1 teaspoon baking soda
- ½ teaspoon salt

In a large bowl, using an electric beater, mix the butter and icing sugar until light and fluffy. Add the eggs, then the warmed golden syrup, and mix well. Add the rest of the ingredients and mix thoroughly. Wrap in cling film and refrigerate until firm, ideally about 2 hours.

Preheat the oven to 180°C. Line a baking tray with baking paper.

On a lightly floured board roll the dough to 3–5 mm thickness and cut with cookie cutters. Transfer to the prepared tray.

Bake for 10–15 minutes. The cookies should be just colouring brown at the edges. Cool for 5 minutes on the tray, then transfer to a wire rack. Ice and decorate when cold. Store in an airtight container.

Prep time 10 minutes plus icing
Chill time 2 hours
Cook time 15 minutes

MAKES ABOUT 40 COOKIES
DEPENDING ON THE SHAPE

ROYAL ICING TO DECORATE

- 2 egg whites
- 2 tablespoons cold water
- 1 tablespoon strained fresh lemon juice
- 2½ cups icing sugar
- food colouring (optional)

Beat the egg whites and water together, then add the lemon juice and icing sugar. Mix until smooth. Transfer to a piping bag with a small round nozzle and decorate the cookies as desired.

Note: If I am making them into Christmas tree decorations I make a hole in the dough to thread ribbon through before baking – I use a wooden skewer or firm plastic drinking straw.

SLICES AND BROWNIES

*This is like a white chocolate brownie, and
I love the addition of salted cashews.*

SALTED CASHEW
AND WHITE CHOCOLATE SLICE

- *275 g white chocolate melts (a packet of melts is
  375 g so keep the remaining 100 g for the icing)*
- *250 g butter*
- *1 cup caster sugar*
- *4 eggs*
- *2 teaspoons vanilla*
- *2 cups flour*
- *1 cup salted, roasted cashew nuts*

FOR THE ICING
- *100 g white chocolate melts*
- *50 g butter*
- *1 cup icing sugar*
- *milk to mix*

Preheat the oven to 160°C. Line a 20 x 30 cm slice tin with baking paper.

Melt the white chocolate and butter together and mix until smoothly combined. This can be done in short bursts of 20 seconds in the microwave.

With an electric mixer, beat the sugar, eggs and vanilla until creamy and pale. Add the melted chocolate mixture and the flour, then mix in the cashews. Mix well. Spread the mixture into the prepared tin and bake for 40–45 minutes. The top surface will be golden brown but the centre still quite soft.

Cool completely before icing.

To make the icing, melt the white chocolate and butter together, then mix in the icing sugar with enough milk to make a smooth but thick icing. Spread over the cooled slice and let the icing set before cutting into portions. This freezes well either iced or un-iced.

Prep time 20 minutes
Cook time 45 minutes

MAKES 30 PIECES

This is my Granny Win's recipe. Very quick and simple but such a complex butterscotch flavour. A frequently requested recipe.

Butterscotch Date Fingers

- 250 G BUTTER
- 2½ CUPS BROWN SUGAR
- 2 EGGS
- 2 CUPS SELF-RAISING FLOUR
- 2½ CUPS CHOPPED PITTED DATES
  (CUT EACH DATE INTO 4–5 PIECES)

Preheat the oven to 180°C. Line a 20 x 30 cm slice tin with baking paper.

Place the butter and brown sugar in a medium-sized saucepan and stir over medium heat until the butter melts and the sugar is dissolved. Cool in the saucepan.

When the butter mixture has cooled, pour into a mixing bowl and beat in the eggs, then the flour. Lastly, add the dates and mix well.

Scrape the mixture into the prepared tin and bake for 18–20 minutes until the surface is shiny and dry. Cool in the tin. Cut into fingers when cold. Freezes really well.

Prep time 15 minutes
Cook time 20 minutes

MAKES 24 PIECES

RASPBERRY FUDGE BROWNIE

- *300 g butter, cut into cubes*
- *300 g dark chocolate, roughly chopped*
- *6 eggs*
- *2 cups caster sugar*
- *1½ cups flour*
- *½ cup cocoa*
- *2 teaspoons vanilla*
- *1 cup whole raspberries (can be frozen free-flow raspberries – do not thaw)*
- *extra ½ cup chopped chocolate*

Preheat the oven to 170°C. Line a 25 x 35 cm sponge-roll tin with baking paper.

Melt the butter and chocolate together in the microwave or over a saucepan of simmering water.

Beat the eggs and caster sugar together until pale and creamy. Add the melted butter and chocolate mixture. Sift the flour and cocoa together and mix into the chocolate mixture with the vanilla. Mix until well combined.

Pour into the prepared tin and sprinkle with the raspberries and extra chopped chocolate. There is no need to press these down into the mxture. Bake for 30 minutes, then cool in the tin. Cut into slices when cold. Store in an airtight container – can be frozen.

Prep time 15 minutes
Cook time 30 minutes

MAKES 30 PIECES

We make so many brownies in the café, and this is the favourite.

'Find something you are
passionate about and keep
tremendously interested in it.'

Julia Child

My favourite, and so easy to turn a brownie like this into a scrumptious dessert – just serve warm and add ice cream.

Salted Caramel Fudge Brownie

- 300 G BUTTER, CUT INTO CUBES
- 300 G DARK CHOCOLATE, ROUGHLY CHOPPED
- 6 EGGS
- 2 CUPS CASTER SUGAR
- 1½ CUPS FLOUR
- ½ CUP BAKING COCOA
- 2 TEASPOONS VANILLA
- 1 X 380 G CAN CARAMELISED CONDENSED MILK
- EXTRA ½ CUP CHOPPED CHOCOLATE
- 1 TABLESPOON FLAKY SEA SALT

Preheat the oven to 170°C. Line a 25 x 35 cm sponge-roll tin with baking paper.

Melt the butter and chocolate together in the microwave or over a saucepan of simmering water. Gently heat together, stirring as they melt.

Beat the eggs and caster sugar together until pale and creamy. Add the melted butter and chocolate mixture. Sift the flour and cocoa together and mix into the chocolate with the vanilla. Mix until well combined.

Pour into the prepared tin and sprinkle with teaspoonfuls of caramelised condensed milk, extra chopped chocolate and flaky sea salt. Bake for 30–35 minutes, then cool in the tin. Cut into slices when cold. Store in an airtight container – can be frozen.

Handy tip: When I was a Girl Guide we used to make our own caramel by boiling a can of sweetened condensed milk for 2–3 hours. Do not try to relive your past with the new rip-top cans as they explode and the caramel will be everywhere – ceiling, curtains, etc. If you really like to make your own version, tip the can into a small bowl and place that in a slow cooker overnight or for about 6 hours to reach the gooey caramel consistency required.

Prep time 15 minutes
Cook time 35 minutes

MAKES 30 PIECES

I love the classic taste of Cherry Ripe bars. This is my version.

CHOCOLATE CHERRY SLICE

- *300 g dark chocolate, broken into cubes or bite-sized pieces*
- *1 egg*
- *½ cup caster sugar*
- *2 cups chopped glacé cherries (approximately 300 g)*
- *1 cup coconut*

Preheat the oven to 180°C. Line a 20 x 30 cm slice tin with baking paper.

Scatter the chocolate pieces in the prepared tin. Place the tin in the oven for 6–7 minutes to melt the chocolate.

Using a spatula, spread the chocolate evenly around the base of the tin. Cool in the fridge.

Beat the egg and caster sugar together, then mix in the cherries and coconut.

Spoon over the chocolate. Bake for 20 minutes. Cool in the tin, then chill in the fridge before cutting into slices.

Prep time 20 minutes
Cook time 20 minutes

MAKES 24 PIECES

This has a double-thick layer of gooey caramel under the dark chocolate topping. Who doesn't love this part of a caramel slice best?

Extra Gooey Caramel Slice

For the base
- ¾ CUP BROWN SUGAR
- 1½ CUPS FLOUR
- ½ CUP COCONUT
- 200 G BUTTER, MELTED

For the filling
- 125 G BUTTER
- ⅓ CUP GOLDEN SYRUP
- 2 X 400 G CANS SWEETENED CONDENSED MILK

For the topping
- 1 X 375 G PACKET DARK CHOCOLATE MELTS

Preheat the oven to 180°C. Line a 20 x 30 cm slice tin with baking paper.

Mix the base ingredients together and press the mixture into the prepared tin. Bake for 15–18 minutes until lightly browned.

Combine the filling ingredients in a medium-sized saucepan and stir over medium heat until smoothly combined and hot. Pour over the warm base and bake for a further 20 minutes until golden brown. Cool in the tin.

Melt the chocolate according to the packet instructions, then spread over the surface of the cooled slice. Allow to set before cutting into pieces.

Prep time 20 minutes
Cook time 40 minutes

MAKES 20 PIECES

VANILLA AND PASSIONFRUIT CUSTARD SLICE

- *2 sheets frozen puff pastry, thawed*
- *1 cup caster sugar*
- *½ cup cornflour*
- *½ cup custard powder*
- *3 cups milk*
- *300 ml cream*
- *60 g butter, chopped into pieces*
- *2 egg yolks*
- *2 teaspoons vanilla*

FOR THE PASSIONFRUIT TOPPING

- *2½ cups (approximately) icing sugar*
- *25 g butter, softened to room temperature*
- *4 tablespoons passionfruit pulp (about 4 passionfruit, or can be from a jar)*

Preheat the oven to 200°C. Line an oven tray with baking paper. Line the base and sides of a 23 cm square cake tin with baking paper. Allow the paper to overhang the sides by 2–3 cm.

Place the pastry sheets on the prepared oven tray and bake for 12–15 minutes until puffed and golden. Leave the pastry sheets to cool on the tray, covered with a clean tea towel. Gently flatten the pastry if it has puffed up unevenly. When cool, trim a sheet of pastry to fit the prepared cake tin and line the base. I find a small serrated bread knife best for this trimming job.

In a medium-sized saucepan, stir the sugar, cornflour, custard powder, milk and cream together. Whisk continuously over medium heat until it thickens. Add the butter, whisking to smoothly combine. Reduce the temperature and beat in the egg yolks and vanilla.

Mix until well combined, then pour into the cake tin, smoothing the surface. Top with the second pastry sheet, trimmed to fit, press it down gently, and then chill the slice for 2–3 hours.

To make the topping, beat the icing sugar, butter and passionfruit pulp together until smooth. Depending on the amount of passionfruit, you may need more or less icing sugar. Spread over the chilled slice, then chill again until the topping has set.

Lift out of the tin using the overhanging baking paper as handles. Slice into pieces. A serrated knife is useful to cut neatly through the pastry sheets. Wipe the knife after each cut. Keep refrigerated, and best eaten within 2 days.

Prep time 25 minutes
Cook time 15 minutes
Chill time 2–3 hours

MAKES 16 PIECES

A VERY POPULAR CAFÉ SLICE
THAT WILL SOON
HAVE A BIG FOLLOWING
IN YOUR HOME.

You either love them or hate them – Bounty Bars. Here's a great slice if you're a lover of them like me.

Bounty Bar Chocolate Slice

- 2 X 45 G BOUNTY BARS
- 150 G DARK CHOCOLATE, CHOPPED
- 75 G BUTTER
- 1 EGG
- ¼ CUP CASTER SUGAR
- ½ CUP BROWN SUGAR
- ¾ CUP FLOUR
- ½ CUP SWEETENED CONDENSED MILK
- 1½ CUPS COCONUT
- 2 TEASPOONS COCONUT ESSENCE
- 1 X 375 G PACKET DARK CHOCOLATE MELTS

Preheat the oven to 160°C. Line a 10 x 20 x 7 cm deep loaf tin with baking paper, allowing the edges to overhang the tin.

Chop the Bounty Bars into small 1 cm pieces. Place the Bounty Bar pieces, dark chocolate and butter in a small saucepan and melt together over gentle heat. Mix well, then allow to cool slightly.

In an electric mixer, beat the egg and sugars together until well combined and pale and creamy. Add the cooled chocolate mixture. Add the flour and mix until smooth. Pour into the prepared loaf tin. Bake for 25 minutes. Leave the oven on, but remove the tin to cool on a wire rack for 5 minutes.

Mix the condensed milk, coconut and essence together. Spoon this over the cooling base in the loaf tin, spreading out evenly.

Bake for a further 20–25 minutes until lightly golden. Cool completely in the tin.

When cold, melt the dark chocolate melts and pour over the top of the slice, smoothing evenly. Chill until the chocolate has set. Use the overhanging paper like handles to remove the slice from the tin. Cut into even-sized slices or bars.

Keeps in an airtight container in the fridge for a week (if you're lucky and it hasn't been raided).

Prep time 15 minutes
Cook time 50 minutes

MAKES 16–20 PIECES

*A delicious citrusy slice with a fine meringue layer
on top — quite sticky and 'lick your fingers' delicious.*

CLEMENTINE SLICE

FOR THE BASE
- 1½ cups flour
- ¾ cup caster sugar
- 150 g butter, cut into cubes

FOR THE TOPPING
- 4 eggs
- 1¾ cups caster sugar
- grated rind of 2 lemons
- grated rind of 2 oranges
- ½ cup lemon juice
- ¼ cup orange juice
- ⅓ cup flour
- icing sugar, to dust

Preheat the oven to 180°C. Line a 20 x 30 cm slice tin with baking paper.

Place the base ingredients in a food processor and run the machine until the pastry clumps around the blade. Press into the base of the prepared tin and bake for 15 minutes until dry-looking and lightly golden brown.

Reduce the oven temperature to 160°C.

Without washing the food processor, whiz up the eggs, caster sugar and lemon and orange rind until really frothy. Add the juices and flour and pulse to just combine.

Carefully pour over the hot base and return to the oven for 35–40 minutes until the filling is set.

Cool in the tin, then lift out and dust with icing sugar, then slice into pieces. Store in an airtight container for 3–4 days. Can be frozen.

Prep time 10 minutes
Cook time 55 minutes

MAKES 20–24 PIECES

Pascall

CADBURY FRY HUDSON LTD.

This is lovely and crunchy, not at all cakey, and it has a thin layer of gingery topping, not an icing. Ginger lovers will adore it. This is Ginger Crunch like Granny used to make – not the iced shortcake slice so often served in cafés as a pretend Ginger Crunch.

Really Crunchy & Gingery Ginger Crunch

For the base
- 100 G BUTTER, CUT INTO CUBES, SOFTENED
- ¾ CUP CASTER SUGAR
- 1¼ CUPS FLOUR
- 1 TEASPOON BAKING POWDER
- 2 TABLESPOONS GROUND GINGER

For the topping
- 125 G BUTTER
- 2 TABLESPOONS GOLDEN SYRUP
- 1 CUP ICING SUGAR
- 1 TABLESPOON GROUND GINGER

Preheat the oven to 180°C. Line a 20 x 30 cm slice tin with baking paper.

In a large bowl, beat the butter and sugar with an electric beater until fluffy and pale. Mix in the flour, baking powder and ground ginger. Mix well. This will be quite a crumbly mixture. Press into the prepared tin and bake for 15 minutes until lightly golden brown.

While the base is cooking, melt the butter and golden syrup for the topping in a small saucepan.

Using a wire whisk, whisk in the icing sugar and ground ginger and beat until smooth. Pour over the hot slice, spreading to the edges with a spatula. Cool in the tin, then in the fridge. When the topping is properly set, remove from the tin and slice into pieces. Store in an airtight container for up to a week.

Prep time 5 minutes
Cook time 15 minutes

MAKES 20–24 PIECES

Count the memories,
not the calories.

Emily worked with me in the Cook School and is fondly remembered, especially when we make her Lemon Shortcake which has a big following here in Oxford.

EMILY'S LEMON SHORTCAKE

FOR THE PASTRY

- 1½ cups self-raising flour
- 1½ cups flour
- 1½ cups sugar
- 150 g butter, cold, and grated or finely diced
- 2 eggs, beaten
- 3 tablespoons milk

FOR THE FILLING

- 100 g butter
- grated rind and juice of 3 lemons
- 1 cup caster sugar
- 3 eggs, beaten
- icing sugar, to dust

Preheat the oven to 180°C. Line a 20 x 30 cm slice tin with baking paper.

Place the flours and sugar in an electric-mixer bowl and mix together, then add the butter and run the machine to combine. Add the beaten eggs and milk and mix until a dough forms. Divide off a third of the dough, wrap in cling film and chill in the fridge. Press the remaining dough into the lined tin and bake for 8–10 minutes until lightly golden and just cooked.

While the pastry is cooking, prepare the filling. Place the butter, lemon rind and juice, and the caster sugar in a saucepan over low heat. Stir until the sugar is dissolved.

Add the beaten eggs and continue to stir until the mixture starts to thicken, but is not yet boiling. Pour the lemon filling over the partially cooked shortcake.

Cut walnut-sized pieces of the refrigerated dough, press flat in your hand and dot all over the lemon filling. Bake a further 10–15 minutes until the shortcake is lightly golden brown. Cool in the tin, then cut into squares. Serve generously dusted with icing sugar. Keeps in an airtight container for 2–3 days but not very good to freeze.

Prep time 10 minutes
Cook time 25 minutes

MAKES 20–24 PIECES

My very elderly Great Aunt Annie made this in the coal range. We always got a slice when we filled her 'chip tin' with kindling wood for her. It was a Sunday afternoon chore – and treat. I have quite a few old bowls, wire cooling racks and kitchen bits and pieces that came from Aunt Annie's so she is often in my kitchen memories.

Aunt Annie's Louise Cake

For the base
- **100 G BUTTER**
- **¼ CUP CASTER SUGAR**
- **3 EGGS, SEPARATED**
- **1¾ CUPS FLOUR**
- **2 TEASPOONS BAKING POWDER**

For the filling
- **1 CUP RASPBERRY JAM**

For the topping
- **¾ CUP CASTER SUGAR**
- **¾ CUP COCONUT**

Preheat the oven to 180°C. Line a 20 x 30 cm slice tin with baking paper.

Melt the butter. I do this in a large bowl in the microwave. Whisk in the caster sugar, then the egg yolks, keeping the egg whites for the topping. Mix in the flour and baking powder. Spread the mixture into the prepared tin, evenly pressing it in. Spread the jam evenly over the base.

With an electric mixer, beat the egg whites until stiff. Add the caster sugar and coconut and mix together. Spread this over the jam-covered base. Bake for 20–25 minutes until the topping is golden and the slice cooked through. Cool in the tin, then remove to slice. Keeps in an airtight container for 2–3 days.

Tip: When melting butter in a microwave, I leave the paper on as this stops it splattering all over the inside of the microwave. Just remember to fish it out before carrying on with the instructions – and also, don't do this with foil-wrapped butter.

Prep time 10 minutes
Cook time 25 minutes

MAKES 20 PIECES

This is really a delicious treat and shouldn't be part of your daily diet. Very much for 'special occasions' only but also a very requested popular recipe.

CARAMEL OATY SLICE

FOR THE BASE
- 2 cups flour
- 1 cup self-raising flour
- 1 cup coconut
- 2 cups brown sugar
- 3 cups rolled oats (we use wholegrain rolled oats; they are more rounded and less flattened than normal rolled oats)
- 2 eggs
- 300 g butter, melted

FOR THE FILLING
- 200 g butter
- 2 x 400 g cans condensed milk
- 4 tablespoons (¼ cup) golden syrup
- 1 teaspoon vanilla
- white chocolate melts, to decorate, and icing sugar, to dust (optional)

Preheat the oven to 180°C. Line a 25 x 35 cm slice or sponge-roll tin with baking paper. Make sure the paper has a good overhang.

To make the base, combine the dry ingredients in a bowl. Add the eggs and the melted butter. Mix well, then press two-thirds of the mixture into the prepared tin.

For the filling, slowly melt the butter, condensed milk and golden syrup together in a medium-sized saucepan over medium heat. Mix well, then add the vanilla. Pour onto the base.

Sprinkle the remaining crumbly base on top of the filling and bake for 18–20 minutes. Cool and refrigerate. Best to cut the next day, to get beautiful slices.

Can be drizzled with melted white chocolate and dusted with icing sugar to decorate. This slice keeps in an airtight container but is best eaten in 3–4 days – usually not a problem.

Prep time 10 minutes
Cook time 20 minutes

MAKES 20–24 PIECES

This is an old family favourite and a great way of using up a good crop of rhubarb. It is an easy dessert served warm with cream or yoghurt and a good dusting of icing sugar.

Rhubarb Spicetail Slice

For the base
- 125 G BUTTER
- ½ CUP SUGAR
- 1 EGG
- 1½ CUPS SELF-RAISING FLOUR

For the topping
- ¼ CUP FLOUR
- 1½ CUPS CASTER SUGAR
- 2 EGGS
- 3 CUPS FINELY CHOPPED RHUBARB STALKS
- 1½ TEASPOONS MIXED SPICE
- ICING SUGAR, TO DUST

Preheat the oven to 180°C. Line a 20 x 30 cm slice tin with baking paper, leaving a generous overhang.

To make the base, mix the butter and sugar together in a food processor, then add the egg and the self-raising flour. Press the mixture into the prepared tin.

For the topping, mix the flour, sugar and eggs together in the food processor. Add the rhubarb and spice, and pulse until just combined. Don't overprocess the chopped rhubarb.

Cover the base with topping and bake for 30–35 minutes until firm and set. Cool in the tin. Using the overhang as handles, remove from the tin and dust with icing sugar. Serve with cream or yoghurt. Keeps in an airtight container for 3–4 days.

Prep time 15 minutes
Cook time 35 minutes

MAKES 20–24 PIECES

This was a recipe that got its name from workmen who said, 'Thanks for the bloody good fudge slice,' which they'd been given for morning tea.

BLOODY GOOD FUDGE SLICE

- *150 g butter*
- *2 tablespoons golden syrup*
- *1 cup sugar*
- *1 cup coconut*
- *2 cups flour*
- *1 cup sultanas*
- *¾ cup chopped walnuts*

FOR THE CHOCOLATE ICING

- *2 cups icing sugar*
- *3 tablespoons cocoa*
- *25 g butter, melted*
- *boiling water to mix*

Preheat the oven to 150°C. Line a 20 x 30 cm slice tin with baking paper.

Melt the butter in a large microwave bowl. Mix in the golden syrup, then add the dry ingredients. Mix well and press into the prepared tin.

Bake for 10–12 minutes. Cool in the tin before icing.

To make the icing, mix all the ingredients together, adding enough boiling water to make a smooth paste. Spread over the cooled slice and cut it into pieces. Keeps in an airtight container for 7–10 days.

Prep time 10 minutes
Cook time 12 minutes

MAKES 20–24 PIECES

I've been making this for years and years and it always proves very popular. A great thing to take for a coffee morning or office shout.

Cappuccino Date Slice

- 2 EGGS
- 1 CUP BROWN SUGAR
- 180 G BUTTER, MELTED
- ½ CUP MILK
- 2 TABLESPOONS SWEETENED COFFEE & CHICORY ESSENCE (AVAILABLE IN THE COFFEE SECTION OF THE SUPERMARKET)
- 1 CUP DATES, PITTED AND CHOPPED INTO SMALL PIECES (CUT EACH DATE INTO 4–5 PIECES)
- 1½ CUPS FLOUR
- 2 TEASPOONS BAKING POWDER

For the coffee icing
- 2 CUPS ICING SUGAR
- 1 TABLESPOON SWEETENED COFFEE & CHICORY ESSENCE
- 25 G BUTTER, MELTED
- BOILING WATER TO MIX

Preheat the oven to 150°C. Line a 20 x 30 cm slice tin with baking paper.

Beat the eggs in a large bowl, add all the other slice ingredients and mix well to thoroughly combine. Spread into the prepared tin and bake for 20–25 minutes. Cool in the tin.

Mix all the icing ingredients together, adding enough boiling water to form a smooth, glossy, spreadable icing. Spread over the cooled slice. When cold, cut into 30 slices.

Prep time 10 minutes
Cook time 25 minutes

MAKES 30 PIECES

The quaint old-fashioned tradition of afternoon tea can move with the times.

My friend Deb gave me this recipe years ago and we love it. It makes lots but because it is so rich you only need small pieces. If you camouflage it in the fridge it keeps very well — otherwise you'll find it slowly disappearing as people sneak little nibbles, piece by piece.

DEB'S PEPPERMINT CHOCOLATE SLICE

FOR THE BASE
- 125 g butter
- 3 tablespoons cocoa
- ½ cup caster sugar
- 1 egg
- 1 teaspoon vanilla
- 1 cup coconut
- ½ cup chopped walnuts
- 2 cups biscuit crumbs (wine, digestive, etc.)

FOR THE MINT LAYER
- 4 tablespoons Kremelta, melted
- ¼ cup milk
- 2 cups icing sugar
- 1½ teaspoons peppermint essence

FOR THE TOPPING
- 50 g butter
- 250 g dark chocolate melts or chocolate chips

Line a 20 x 30 cm slice tin with baking paper.

In a medium-sized saucepan combine the butter, cocoa and sugar and stir over gentle heat until the sugar is dissolved. Remove from the heat and beat in the egg and vanilla, then mix in the coconut, walnuts and biscuit crumbs and press into the prepared tin. Chill for at least an hour.

Mix all of the mint layer ingredients together until smooth and spread over the chilled base. Return to the fridge to set and chill for a further 30–40 minutes.

To make the topping, melt the butter and chocolate together until smooth, mixing gently, then spread over the chilled slice.

Return to the fridge then cut into pieces when cold and set. This can be stored in an airtight tin but is especially good if served cold from the fridge. Wonderful with coffee in lieu of dessert.

Note: The only time people have trouble with this recipe is when they have used a cheap generic icing sugar. Stick to a quality gluten-free icing sugar that doesn't have a floury additive like wheaten cornflour.

Prep time 15 minutes
Chill time 2 hours

MAKES 40 PIECES

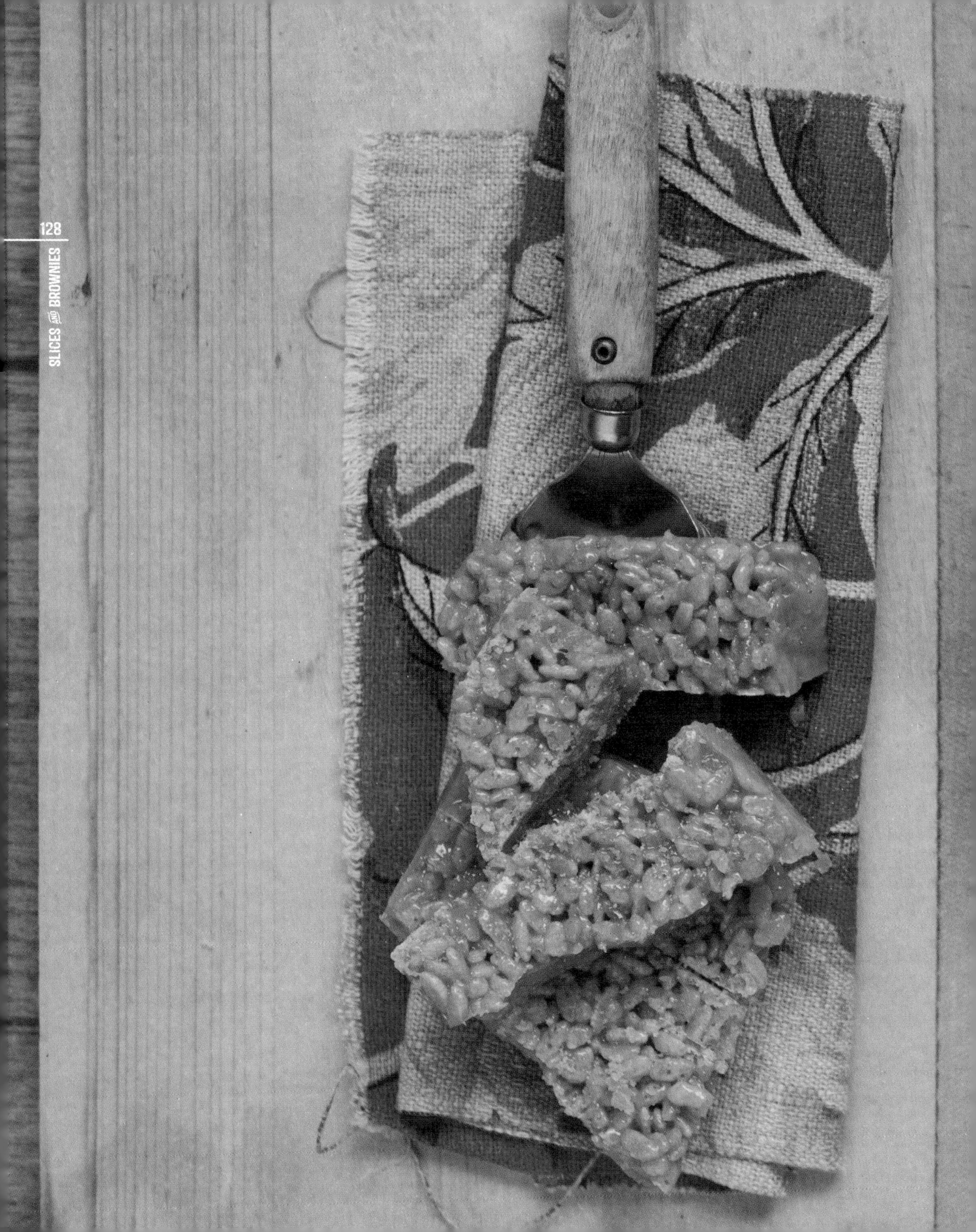

This was a birthday party favourite when I was a girl and is a blast from my childhood. I always like this honey version better than the popular chocolate version. It is not so good for people with dodgy teeth, but dentists love it for business.

Honey Crunch Rice Bubble Slice

- 375 G BUTTER
- 6 TABLESPOONS HONEY
- 3 CUPS SUGAR
- 6 CUPS RICE BUBBLE-TYPE CEREAL

Line a 20 x 30 cm slice tin with baking paper.

Place the butter, honey and sugar in a large saucepan. Stir over medium heat until the sugar is dissolved and the mixture comes up to a good boil.

Remove from the heat and stir in the rice bubbles. Press into the prepared tin and leave to set. Mark into squares.

When completely cold, remove from the tin and cut along the marked lines. Store in an airtight container for up to 10 days.

Prep time 10 minutes
Chill time 1 hour

MAKES 30–36 PIECES

This was my dad's favourite.

COCONUT ROUGH

FOR THE SLICE
- *1½ cups self-raising flour*
- *1 cup sugar*
- *1½ cups coconut*
- *3 tablespoons cocoa*
- *200 g butter, melted*

FOR THE CHOCOLATE ICING
- *2 tablespoons hot water*
- *25 g butter*
- *2 cups icing sugar*
- *2 tablespoons cocoa*
- *extra ¼ cup coconut, to sprinkle*

Preheat the oven to 180°C. Line a 20 x 30 cm slice tin with baking paper.

Mix all the slice ingredients together in a large bowl. Press into the prepared tin and bake for 20 minutes. Cool in the tin while you make the icing.

For the icing, place the water and butter in a microwave-proof jug or small bowl. Heat in the microwave on high for 30–40 seconds until the butter is melted. Beat in the icing sugar and cocoa until smooth, adding a little extra water if required.

Spread the icing over the coconut rough while it's still warm and in the tin. Sprinkle over some extra coconut and cut into slices, but leave to set and go completely cold in the tin before removing. Store in an airtight container for up to 10 days. This freezes well.

Prep time 15 minutes
Cook time 20 minutes

MAKES 24–30 PIECES

My mother Fay's famous Mumbles. This recipe has been sent all over the world and remains a central part of our family's baking folklore. It can be prepared, baked and eaten in half an hour. This is a great way to use up the end of a box of Weet-Bix or cereal.

Fay's Mumbles

- 125 G BUTTER
- 1 CUP SUGAR
- 2 TABLESPOONS GOLDEN SYRUP
- 1 CUP FLOUR
- 1 TEASPOON BAKING POWDER
- 1 CUP COCONUT
- 1 EGG
- 1 CUP MIXED DRIED FRUIT (RAISINS, CURRANTS, ETC.)
- 5 WEET-BIX OR EQUIVALENT DRY WHOLE-WHEAT BREAKFAST CEREAL, CRUSHED

Preheat the oven to 180°C. Line a 20 x 30 cm slice tin with baking paper.

Melt the butter, sugar and golden syrup in a large saucepan over medium heat. Add all the other ingredients and mix thoroughly. Press into the prepared tin. Bake for 15–20 minutes.

Cut into bars while still warm. Store in an airtight container for 10–14 days. Can be frozen.

Prep time 5 minutes
Cook time 20 minutes

MAKES 20 PIECES

MARS BAR BUBBLE SLICE

- *3 x 53 g Mars Bars, chopped into small pieces*
- *100 g butter*
- *1 tablespoon cocoa*
- *3 cups rice bubble-type cereal*
- *1 x 375 g packet milk chocolate melts*

Melt the chopped Mars Bars and butter together in a large bowl in the microwave on medium or 50% power for 3–4 minutes, stirring several times, until melted and well combined. Stir in the cocoa and rice bubble cereal and mix well to combine.

Press into the prepared tin. Refrigerate until solid and chilled.

Heat the milk chocolate in a microwave-proof bowl on medium or 50% power, stirring every 30 seconds until smooth and melted. Spread over the chilled slice and return to the fridge to set. Cut into bars and store in an airtight container in the fridge.

Prep time 10 minutes
Chill time 1 hour

MAKES 30 PIECES

THIS IS A QUICK TREAT AND ALWAYS
GOES DOWN WELL IF GIVEN AS A GIFT
OR IN A 'BRING A PLATE' SITUATION.

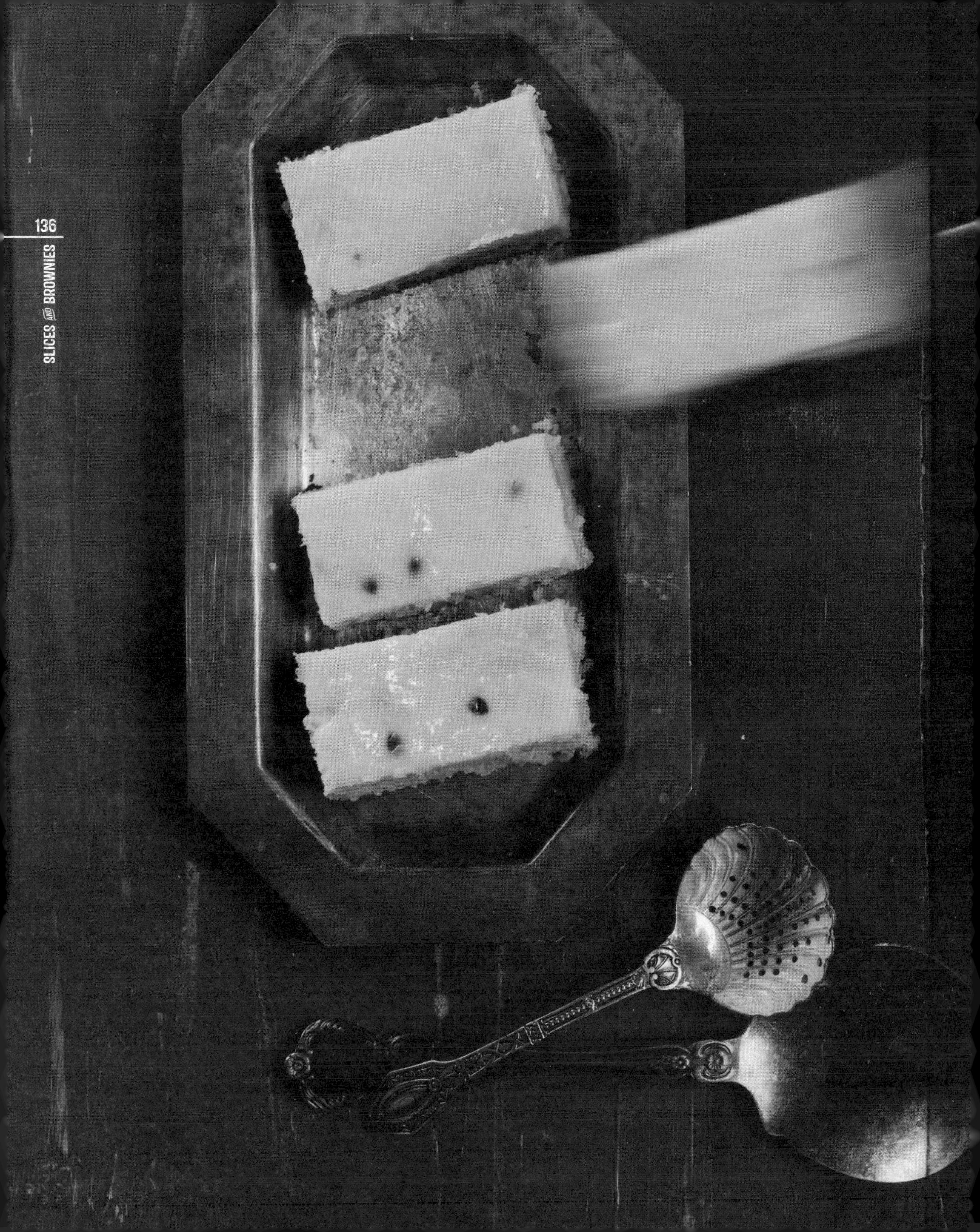

A very popular slice in our café, and I always had to send this back to boarding school with my kids.

Passionfruit & Lemon Slice

For the base
- 2 CUPS COCONUT
- 2 CUPS SELF-RAISING FLOUR
- 1 CUP CASTER SUGAR
- 250 G BUTTER, MELTED

For the passionfruit & lemon layer
- 1 X 400 G CAN SWEETENED CONDENSED MILK
- GRATED RIND OF 2 LEMONS
- ½ CUP LEMON JUICE
- ¼ CUP PASSIONFRUIT PULP
  (ABOUT 4 PASSIONFRUIT, OR CAN BE FROM A JAR)

Preheat the oven to 180°C. Line a 20 x 30 cm slice tin with baking paper.

Place the coconut, flour and sugar in the bowl of an electric mixer. Run the machine as you pour in the melted butter, and mix well. Press the mixture into the base of the prepared tin. Bake for 12–15 minutes until very lightly golden. Remove from the oven but leave the oven on.

Combine the condensed milk, lemon rind and juice, and passionfruit pulp. Spread over the warm base and return to the oven for 10–12 minutes. Cool. This is best chilled for a few hours or overnight before slicing into bars. I keep it in an airtight container and store it in the fridge.

Prep time 10 minutes
Cook time 30 minutes

MAKES 24 BARS OR PIECES

CAKES

Fluffy, white and impressive. This is a big crowd-pleasing but dead-easy cake to make. Replacing the flour with a gluten-free baking mix makes this a fabulous treat for someone on a gluten-free diet, and it's almost fat free as well.

ANGEL FOOD CAKE
▸ GLUTEN FREE

- ¾ cup caster sugar
- 1 cup flour (or GF baking mix)
- 12 egg whites (approximately 2 cups of egg white)
- 1 teaspoon cream of tartar
- ¼ teaspoon salt
- extra ¾ cup caster sugar
- 2 teaspoons vanilla

Preheat the oven to 160°C. Have an Angel Food Cake tin at the ready – this is NOT to be sprayed or greased in any way and does not require any lining with baking paper.

Sift the first ¾ cup of caster sugar and the flour 3 times to really aerate it, then set aside.

Place the egg whites, cream of tartar and salt in a large bowl (preferably metal, glass or china – not plastic). Using an electric beater, beat until soft peaks form. Gradually add the second measure of ¾ cup caster sugar and beat until the mixture is thick and glossy. Turn the beater to low speed and add the vanilla, then fold in the sifted flour and sugar. Spoon into the Angel Food Cake tin and bang it down a couple of times on the bench to remove any air pockets.

Bake for 35–40 minutes until dry-textured and golden brown. Turn upside down and cool on the bench inverted until cold.

Do not try to remove the cake from the tin before 2–3 hours minimum. Just let it cool upside down. This is very important.

When cold, run a knife around the edge of the tin and carefully lift off the base. Slice with a serrated knife.

This cake can be sliced into 3 layers and filled with butter cream frosting (see page 290) or cream, or lemon curd (see page 293).

Slices of Angel Food Cake can be frozen and a quick dessert made by grilling or toasting a slice and serving with fresh or canned fruit.

Note: It is important not to grease the tin as this prevents the cake rising and gripping the tin's sides. Removing it is easy when cold.

Prep time 10 minutes
Cook time 40 minutes
Cooling time 3 hours

SERVES 12–16

This is an easy apple cake, rich with spices, that has the whole house smelling like apple pie. Great for a quick dessert. Especially loved by the boys in my family.

Cloves & Cinnamon Apple Cake

- 150 G BUTTER, MELTED
- 1 X 500 G CAN APPLE PIE FILLING, OR 2 BIG CUPS FIRM, DRAINED STEWED APPLE (DON'T LET IT BE TOO WET A MIXTURE)
- 1 CUP BROWN SUGAR
- 2 EGGS
- 2 CUPS FLOUR
- 2 TEASPOONS CINNAMON
- 1 TEASPOON GROUND CLOVES
- 2 TEASPOONS BAKING POWDER
- ½ CUP RAISINS
- ½ CUP CHOPPED WALNUTS OR PECANS (OPTIONAL)
- ICING SUGAR, TO DUST

Preheat the oven to 160°C. Spray a 20–21cm spring-form tin or Bundt tin with baking spray and, if using a spring-form tin, line the base with baking paper.

Place the melted butter in a large bowl, then add all the other ingredients and mix well. Pour into the prepared tin and bake for 55–60 minutes. The surface will be golden brown and firm and the edges will be pulling away from the sides of the tin.

Cool in the tin for 10 minutes, then turn out onto a wire rack to completely cool. Dust with icing sugar to serve. Can be served warm as a dessert with softly whipped cream or yoghurt.

Prep time 5 minutes
Cook time 60 minutes

SERVES 10–12

SEAGARS CLASSIC BANANA CAKE

- *1½ cups sugar*
- *150 g butter, softened to room temperature*
- *4 eggs*
- *3 bananas, mashed with a fork*
- *¾ cup milk*
- *1 teaspoon baking soda*
- *200 ml plain, thick Greek-style yoghurt*
- *2½ cups flour*
- *3 teaspoons baking powder*

Preheat the oven to 160°C. Spray a 22–23cm round spring-form tin with baking spray. Line the base with baking paper.

Beat the sugar and softened butter together until creamy and pale. Add the eggs and beat until thick and creamy and well incorporated. Add the mashed bananas and mix in well.

Heat the milk in a small saucepan or microwave-proof bowl until nearly boiling.

Stir the baking soda into the milk and then stir this into the banana mixture.

Add the yoghurt, flour and baking powder. Mix well and pour into the prepared cake tin. Bake for 50–60 minutes until the cake is cooked in the middle and just pulling away from the edges of the tin. Cool in the tin for 5 minutes, then unclip the sides and cool completely on a wire rack. When completely cold, ice with fresh lemon icing (see page 290).

Prep time 15 minutes
Cook time 60 minutes

SERVES 8–10

ALWAYS A FAVOURITE, AND IN MY
OPINION IT HAS TO HAVE LEMON ICING
– NOTHING ELSE WILL DO.

145

This couldn't be easier, and is so delicious. It is often the cake recipe I go to when in a complete hurry – i.e. when unexpected guests pop in for afternoon tea. No need to ice it, just dust with icing sugar to serve. It is ready to eat in less than an hour. It is also fat free.

Apricot Cake

- 1 X 400 G CAN APRICOT HALVES IN JUICE
- 2 CUPS SELF-RAISING FLOUR
- 1 CUP SUGAR
- 1 TEASPOON MIXED SPICE
- 1 CUP CHOPPED DRIED APRICOTS
- ICING SUGAR, TO DUST

Preheat the oven to 180°C. Spray a 20–21cm round spring-form tin with baking spray and line the base with baking paper.

Place the contents of the can of apricots, including the juice, in a food processor and whizz until puréed. Add the other ingredients and pulse to mix together. Pour into the prepared tin and bake for 30–35 minutes.

Serve dusted with icing sugar, or it can be iced with cream cheese frosting (see page 293) – obviously this is not in the fat-free category.

Prep time 10 minutes
Cook time 35 minutes

 SERVES 8–10

New Zealand Fr

PE

CHOICE
EXTRA
STANDAR
HEAVY S

PACKED AT THE F

NEW ZEAL

C
C

PACKED AT FRIMLEY
HASTINGS, HAWKES B

APP

CHES

Frimley Brand

CANNING FACTORY, HASTINGS, H.B.

DFRUIT

ES

PIE FRUITS

This is a popular gluten-free café cake. We often substitute peaches or nectarines for the apples and pears.

SPICY APPLE *AND* PEAR CAKE

➤ **GLUTEN FREE**

- 3 eggs
- 1 cup brown sugar
- ½ cup oil
- 1 teaspoon vanilla
- ½ cup raisins or sultanas
- 2 cups raw apples, grated or finely diced (I don't usually peel the fruit)
- 2 cups raw pears, grated or finely diced
- 2 cups gluten-free flour baking mix
- ½ teaspoon salt
- 1 teaspoon baking soda
- 1 teaspoon baking powder
- 1 teaspoon cinnamon

There are numerous recipes and adaptations for Carrot Cake. I think this is the best, and we use it all the time in our café.

Carrot Cake

- 2 CUPS SELF-RAISING FLOUR
- 1 CUP BROWN SUGAR
- 1 TEASPOON BAKING SODA
- ¾ CUP COCONUT
- ¼ CUP CHOPPED WALNUTS, PLUS EXTRA TO GARNISH
- 2 TEASPOONS MIXED SPICE
- ½ CUP SULTANAS
- 2 CUPS GRATED CARROT (2–3 SMALL CARROTS)
- 3 EGGS
- 1 CUP OIL
- 2 TEASPOONS VANILLA ESSENCE
- 1 X 225 G CAN CRUSHED PINEAPPLE, INCLUDING THE LIQUID (EITHER JUICE OR SYRUP)

Preheat the oven to 180°C. Line the base and sides of a 22–23 cm cake tin with baking paper.

Place all the ingredients in a large bowl and mix together until well combined. Spoon into the prepared cake tin and bake for 55–60 minutes until the centre springs back when pressed and the cake is pulling away from the sides of the tin.

Cool on a wire rack and, when cold, ice with cream cheese frosting (see page 293). Decorate with chopped walnuts.

Prep time 15 minutes
Cook time 60 minutes

SERVES 8–10

This is a lovely yellow buttery custard-tasting cake that always looks really impressive. I often serve it with thick yoghurt or cream and some fresh fruit such as strawberries. It is very much a cake-fork cake – perfect for a smart afternoon tea or dessert.

VANILLA CUSTARD CHIFFON CAKE

- 1¼ cups self-raising flour
- 1 teaspoon cream of tartar
- ¼ cup custard powder
- 6 eggs, separated
- 1½ cups caster sugar
- 2 teaspoons vanilla
- ⅓ cup light oil
- ⅔ cup warm water
- icing sugar, to dust

Preheat the oven to 180°C. You need an Angel Food Cake tin, but no preparation is required. Do not spray or line the tin.

Sift the flour, cream of tartar and custard powder together to really mix and aerate them. With an electric mixer, beat the egg whites in a glass, china or metal bowl (not plastic) until frothy. Slowly add ½ cup of caster sugar, one spoonful at a time, until the egg whites are stiff and the sugar is well incorporated. Set aside.

With the electric mixer, in a new bowl, beat the egg yolks together with the remaining cup of caster sugar until pale and creamy. Add the vanilla, then turn the machine to low and mix in the flour, oil and warm water, beating until it is just incorporated. Do not overmix.

Carefully fold the egg-white mixture into the flour mixture, then pour into the Angel

Food Cake tin. Bake for 55–60 minutes until the cake is springy when pressed.

Remove from the oven and immediately turn the cake tin upside down to cool completely. Do not try to remove the cake from the tin until it is completely cool, about 2–3 hours. As with an Angel Food Cake, suspending it upside down prevents the cake from collapsing as it cools.

When cold, run a knife around the outside of the cake and around the centre funnel. Lift off the base of the tin and carefully ease the cake free. Dust with icing sugar to serve.

Prep time 10 minutes
Cook time 60 minutes
Cooling time 3 hours

SERVES 10–12

Soonafai's huge big chocolate cake is a real winner. In fact, I judged it Best Chocolate Cake in New Zealand in a baking competition some years ago. With a few little tweaks I have been making this cake ever since for birthdays and celebrations. It is a great cake for feeding a crowd.

Soonafai's Chocolate Cake

- 2 CUPS SUGAR
- 3 CUPS SELF-RAISING FLOUR
- 2 TEASPOONS BAKING SODA
- ½ CUP COCOA
- 3 EGGS, SEPARATED
- 2 CUPS MILK
- 2 TABLESPOONS MALT VINEGAR
- 2 TABLESPOONS GOLDEN SYRUP
- 2 TEASPOONS VANILLA
- 1½ CUPS COOKING OIL
- 1 WHOLE EGG
- WHIPPED CREAM, RASPBERRY JAM, BERRIES & ICING OF YOUR CHOICE FOR FINISHING

Preheat the oven to 180°C. Spray two 23–26 cm spring-form tins with baking spray and line the bottoms with baking paper.

Combine all the dry ingredients. In a large bowl, preferably glass, metal or china (not plastic), beat the egg whites until stiff.

In a separate bowl, combine the milk and vinegar, then add the rest of the wet ingredients, including the whole egg and the yolks, and beat. Mix the wet and dry ingredients together, then fold in the beaten egg whites.

Pour into the prepared tins and bake for 25–35 minutes. Cool on a wire rack. When cold, carefully slice the cakes horizontally into halves so that you have four layers.

To serve, I generally fill the layers with raspberry jam, whipped cream and berries, then spread the top with chocolate icing (see chocolate butter icing, page 290) and decorate with berries and mint sprigs.

Prep time 15 minutes
Cook time 35 minutes

SERVES 10-12

This isn't just a cake for people following a gluten-free regimen. It is a favourite chocolate cake, one I often serve with berries and cream for dessert.

FLOURLESS CHOCOLATE CAKE
➤ GLUTEN FREE

- 150 g dark chocolate (72% cocoa solids)
- 150 g butter
- 6 eggs, separated
- ¾ cup caster sugar
- 1 cup ground almonds
- ½ cup rice flour
- 2 tablespoons cocoa
- favourite frosting and icing sugar, to dust

Preheat the oven to 160°C. Line the base of a 23-cm spring-form tin with baking paper and spray the paper and sides with baking spray.

Melt the chocolate and butter together, either in the microwave or in a bowl placed over a pan of simmering water, but not actually touching the water – like a double boiler. Stir the chocolate and butter together to smoothly combine.

Beat the egg yolks and sugar together until pale and creamy. Add the ground almonds, rice flour, cocoa and the chocolate mixture and combine.

In a separate glass, china or metal (not plastic) bowl, beat the egg whites until stiff.

Fold the egg whites into the chocolate mixture, then scrape into the prepared tin. Bake for 45–50 minutes. The cake should be dry on the top and firm when gently pressed in the centre, with the sides just pulling away from the tin.

Cool in the tin for 15–20 minutes, then carefully release the sides and turn out to cool on a wire rack. Sometimes the cake does sink a little in the middle, this is normal. Dust with icing sugar (checking that it is GF icing sugar if this is important to you). The cake can also be frosted with pink butter cream or chocolate butter cream (see page 290).

Prep time 15 minutes
Cook time 50 minutes

SERVES 9–12

This recipe has been modified from one found in the archives of our local Oxford Museum. I think it was first developed when the Highlander sweetened condensed milk came on the market. There are no eggs in the recipe and no extra sugar besides what is contained in the sweetened condensed milk.

Seagars at Oxford Christmas Cake

➤ **EGG FREE**

- 1 CUP ORANGE JUICE
- 250 G BUTTER, CUBED
- 1 TABLESPOON CIDER VINEGAR
- 1 KG MIXED DRIED FRUIT
- ½ CUP (1 PACKET) RED GLACÉ CHERRIES
- ½ CUP (1 PACKET) GREEN GLACÉ CHERRIES
- ½ CUP (1 PACKET) MIXED PEEL
- 2 TEASPOONS CINNAMON
- 2 TEASPOONS MIXED SPICE
- 1 TEASPOON GROUND CLOVES
- 1 X 400 G CAN SWEETENED CONDENSED MILK
- 1 TEASPOON BAKING SODA
- 2 TEASPOONS VANILLA
- ½ CUP ORANGE LIQUEUR (COINTREAU, GRAND MARNIER) OR BRANDY
- 2½ CUPS SELF-RAISING FLOUR
- 1 CUP NUTS (BLANCHED ALMONDS, PECANS OR WALNUTS)

Preheat the oven to 150°C. Line the base of a 22–23 cm square spring-form tin with baking paper and spray the sides with baking spray.

Place the orange juice, butter, cider vinegar, mixed fruit, cherries and peel in a large saucepan and bring to the boil. Remove from heat and stir in the spices, condensed milk, soda and vanilla. Add half (¼ cup) the liqueur or brandy and the self-raising flour. Mix well. Stir in the nuts.

Transfer the mixture to the prepared tin and smooth the surface. Bake for 1 hour, then turn the temperature down to 140°C and bake a further 30–50 minutes until the cake feels firm in the centre when pressed and is a deep golden brown.

It should be pulling away from the sides of the tin.

Remove from the oven and pour the remaining ¼ cup of liqueur or brandy over. Cool in the tin, then unclip the sides and remove the cake. Peel off the baking paper and wrap in fresh baking paper and tinfoil and store in a cool place. It can be eaten immediately but will keep well for up to six weeks and can be frozen.

Serve plain, traditionally iced or with brandy butter frosting (see page 290).

Prep time 15 minutes
Cook time 2 hours

MAKES APPROX 20 PIECES

This is quite a major production! Lots of experimenting with mud cake recipes has produced this version. It is a chocolate lovers' dream cake and the most popular dessert in our café. It has a big following. The chocolate mousse and ganache make it the ultimate chocolate cake. You do need to start preparing this cake the day before, but it is so worth it.

SEAGARS CHOCOLATE MUD MOUSSE CAKE

- 1¾ cups flour
- 1¾ cups caster sugar
- 2 teaspoons baking soda
- ¾ cup cocoa
- 1 teaspoon salt
- 1½ cups milk
- 100 g butter, melted
- 2 eggs
- 1 teaspoon vanilla

Preheat the oven to 180°C. Spray a deep 22–23 cm (at least 7–8 cm deep) spring-form cake tin with baking spray and line the base and sides with baking paper.

Mix all the ingredients until smoothly combined. I use the electric mixer for this.

Pour into the prepared tin and bake for 50–55 minutes until firm in the centre when you gently press down, and the cake is pulling away from the sides of the tin. Cool in the tin on a wire rack until completely cold, then carefully remove from the tin. Wash and dry the tin as you need it again to finish preparing the cake.

FOR THE FILLING

- 450 g dark chocolate (72% cocoa solids)
- 2 cups cream
- 6 egg yolks
- ½ cup caster sugar

Place the chocolate and cream in a medium-sized saucepan and heat gently, stirring, until smoothly combined. Cool.

Place the yolks and caster sugar in a bowl over a saucepan of warm water. Beat with a handheld electric mixer on high until the mixture is pale and creamy; this will take 5–6 minutes. Mix in the chocolate and then beat for an additional 5–6 minutes. Chill this mixture for at least 30 minutes.

To assemble

Cut the cooled cake in half horizontally. Line the original cake tin with cling film, allowing a good amount to overhang. Place one half of the cake in the lined tin, then pour in the mousse filling and sandwich the second cake on top. Wrap up in the cling film, covering the top of the cake, and chill in the tin for 8–10 hours or until the next day, before covering with ganache glaze.

FOR THE GANACHE

- *400 g dark chocolate, chopped (50–60% cocoa solids will be sufficient here)*
- *150 ml milk*
- *200 ml cream*

Place all the ingredients in a medium-sized saucepan and stir over gentle heat while the mixture comes up to the boil. Stir as it gently boils, making sure the chocolate is melted and the mixture is smooth. Cool to room temperature, about 2 hours.

Remove the cake from the lined tin and place on a wire rack over a tray to catch the overflow. Gently pour the ganache over the cake, covering the top and down the sides. The overflow can be scraped up and used again to get a thick, even glaze over the entire cake. Put in the fridge to set, then cover loosely with cling film or place in a plastic cake container.

Keep chilled until ready to serve.

Serve with softly whipped cream or ice cream, and berries or fruit and fruit coulis.

Wait for the accolades to pour in. This cake will last really well for a week, therefore it is great to prepare for a wedding or special celebration. Before the cake is covered with the ganache it can be well wrapped and frozen for up to 3 months.

Prep time over 2 days
Cook time 55 minutes

SERVES 10–12, POSSIBLY MANY MORE

This is a moist Canadian cake full of dates and apple with a lovely caramelised coconut topping. A favourite afternoon tea or dessert cake. It is a deep burnished brown and no, you don't have to wear your Swannie and wield an axe to be a fan of its great taste and texture.

Lumberjack Cake

- 2 CUPS PITTED DRIED DATES, ROUGHLY CHOPPED (CUT EACH DATE INTO 4–5 PIECES)
- 1 CUP HOT WATER
- 1 TEASPOON BAKING SODA
- 125 G BUTTER, SOFTENED
- 1¼ CUPS CASTER SUGAR
- 1 EGG, BEATEN
- 1½ CUPS FLOUR
- ½ TEASPOON SALT
- 1 TEASPOON VANILLA
- 2 APPLES, PEELED, CORED & DICED OR GRATED

For the topping
- ¾ CUP BROWN SUGAR
- 60 G BUTTER, SOFTENED
- 1 CUP COARSE THREAD COCONUT
- 4 TABLESPOONS MILK

Preheat the oven to 180°C. Spray a 22–23 cm spring-form tin with baking spray and line with baking paper.

Mix the dates with the hot water and soda, and set aside while you make the remainder of the cake.

Using an electric mixer, beat the butter and sugar in a large bowl until light and fluffy. Slowly beat in the egg. Add the flour, salt and vanilla. Mix in the date mixture, including the liquid, and the chopped apple. Scrape the mixture into the prepared tin and bake for 40–45 minutes or until the top is set and pulls away from the sides of the tin.

Meanwhile, place the topping ingredients in a small saucepan and stir over medium heat until the butter has melted and the ingredients are well combined.

Remove the cake from the oven. Spread the hot topping over to cover the cake and cook for a further 20 minutes or until the topping is golden and the cake is cooked through. Remove from the oven and cool in the tin until ready to serve.

Carefully remove from the tin and lift off the baking paper. This cake is delicious served warm with whipped cream or yoghurt.

Prep time 20 minutes
Cook time 1 hour

SERVES 10–12

KUMARA AND ORANGE CAKE WITH CREAM CHEESE FROSTING

- *3½ cups flour*
- *3 teaspoons baking powder*
- *2 teaspoons baking soda*
- *3 teaspoons cinnamon*
- *3½ cups brown sugar*
- *1½ cups sultanas*
- *1½ cups chopped walnuts*
- *5 cups grated or very finely diced kumara (about 2 large kumara; can be red or golden variety)*
- *5 eggs*
- *350 ml oil*
- *2 tablespoons freshly squeezed orange juice*
- *grated rind of 3 oranges*

Preheat the oven to 180°C. Spray a large, deep 25–26 cm spring-form cake tin with baking spray and line the base with baking paper.

Place all the dry ingredients in a large bowl. Mix in the grated kumara. In a separate bowl beat the eggs, oil, orange juice and rind together, then mix this into the dry ingredients. Pour into the prepared tin and bake for 45–50 minutes, then turn the oven down to 160°C and bake a further 30–35 minutes, until the cake is pulling away from the sides of the tin and is cooked in the middle when tested with a cake skewer. Cool in the tin for 15 minutes before carefully releasing the sides of the spring-form tin and lifting the cake to a wire rack to cool completely.

It is best to store this cake in a covered container in the fridge. Keeps for up to a week.

Prep time 30 minutes
Cook time 1½ hours

SERVES 12–16

CREAM CHEESE FROSTING

- *400 g cream cheese (not softened or low-fat variety)*
- *100 g butter, softened to room temperature*
- *grated rind of 2 oranges*
- *approximately 4 cups icing sugar*

Beat all the ingredients together until whipped smooth and a good spreading consistency, then frost the top and sides of the cake.

THIS IS LIKE A CARROT CAKE BUT WITH A KUMARA AND CITRUS FLAVOURING. IT MAKES A LOVELY NEW ZEALAND CAKE, VERY MOIST AND UNIQUE. A FAVOURITE IN OUR FAMILY AND OFTEN REQUESTED AS A BIRTHDAY CAKE. IT IS QUITE A BIG CAKE SO FEEDS LOTS OF PEOPLE.

This fruit cake is perfect to make for the weekend. It is wonderful to have in the tins for morning and afternoon teas, to share when you read the weekend papers, or just the ticket when you need a cuppa and a piece of cake after mowing the lawns. And no, I haven't missed out any ingredients – it is this simple.

EF
DF

Easy Orange Juice Fruit Cake

➔ EGG & DAIRY FREE

- 1 KG MIXED DRIED FRUIT
- 2 CUPS ORANGE JUICE (FRESHLY SQUEEZED OR FROM A CARTON)
- 2 CUPS SELF-RAISING FLOUR
- 2 TEASPOONS MIXED SPICE

Place the dried fruit in a large bowl and pour over the orange juice. Let this soak for as long as possible – ¾ to 1 hour is ideal, but it can be overnight.

Preheat the oven to 180°C. Spray a 22–23 cm spring-form tin with baking spray and line the base with baking paper.

Stir the flour and mixed spice into the fruit mixture. Combine well. Scrape into the prepared tin and bake for 45 minutes, then reduce the temperature to 160°C and bake a further 35–40 minutes until a skewer inserted into the centre of the cake comes out clean.

The cake should feel firm, with the edges pulling away from the sides of the tin.

Cool in the tin for 15 minutes, then carefully turn out to cool on a wire rack. When cold, wrap in baking paper and store in an airtight container. Can be frozen whole or in slices which are great for lunch boxes.

Prep & soaking time 1 hour
Cook time 1½ hours

MAKES APPROX 20 PIECES

This has literally won lots of prizes for sponge cakes in Women's Institute and A&P shows. It is the best sponge cake I know and never fails to impress.

A PRIZEWINNING SPONGE CAKE

➤ GLUTEN FREE

- 1 cup caster sugar
- 2 tablespoons water
- 4 eggs, separated
- ½ teaspoon vanilla
- 1½ cups GF cornflour
- ½ teaspoon salt
- 1 teaspoon (GF) baking powder

FOR THE FILLING
- jam
- whipped cream
- fresh fruit (optional)
- icing sugar, to dust

Preheat the oven to 180°C. Spray 2 shallow 23-cm sponge tins with baking spray and line the bases with baking paper, then spray the paper too. Note: it is important to use proper shallow sandwich or sponge tins as the cake won't rise properly in a spring-form or deeper tin.

Place the sugar and water in a microwave bowl or small saucepan and bring to the boil. The sugar does not have to dissolve completely.

Beat the egg whites until stiff, then slowly, with the mixer running, dribble in the hot sugar and water solution. Beat really hard. Add the egg yolks and vanilla, then carefully fold in the sifted dry ingredients. Be very gentle with the folding process. Carefully pour into the prepared tins and bake for 18–20 minutes.

As soon as you remove the sponges from the oven, drop the tins from knee height square on the floor – no kidding! This is an odd, but tried and true, sponge trick that 'shocks' the cake and stops it deflating. Cool for 2 minutes in the tins, then turn out onto a wire rack and carefully peel off the paper and cool completely.

When cold, sandwich the two sponges together with jam and whipped cream and, if desired, fruit such as raspberries, strawberries or peach slices. Dust the top with icing sugar. Cut with a serrated knife, wiping the blade after each slice.

Prep time 10 minutes
Cook time 20 minutes

SERVES 8-12

Again, a famous prizewinning recipe from the archives of our Oxford A&P show. I've updated this recipe and added more ginger to enhance the flavour.

A&P Ginger Cake

- 125 G BUTTER
- 1 CUP SUGAR
- 2 EGGS, BEATEN
- ½ CUP GOLDEN SYRUP
- 2 CUPS FLOUR
- ½ TEASPOON SALT
- 1 TEASPOON BAKING POWDER
- 2 TABLESPOONS GROUND GINGER
- 2 TEASPOONS MIXED SPICE
- 1 TEASPOON CINNAMON
- 1 TEASPOON BAKING SODA
- 1 CUP MILK, AT ROOM TEMPERATURE

For the ginger coffee icing
- 3 CUPS ICING SUGAR
- 1 TEASPOON GROUND GINGER
- 1 TEASPOON SWEETENED COFFEE AND CHICORY ESSENCE
- 100 G BUTTER, MELTED
- BOILING WATER, TO MIX

Preheat the oven to 180°C. Spray two 23-cm spring-form cake tins with baking spray and line the base with baking paper.

Beat the butter and sugar together, then add the eggs and golden syrup. Fold in the dry ingredients (not the baking soda). Mix the baking soda and milk together, then stir into the mixture. Pour equally into the 2 prepared tins.

Bake for 30–35 minutes until firm in the centre and pulling away from the sides of the tin. Cool in the tin for 10 minutes, then carefully turn out to cool completely on a wire rack. When completely cold, ice with ginger coffee icing.

To make the icing, sift the icing sugar and ginger together, then beat in the coffee essence and butter. Add a few drops of boiling water to achieve a nice smooth icing consistency.

Place one cake on a serving plate and spread with a thin layer of icing. Sandwich the second cake on top and spread icing on top with a palette knife or spatula.

Prep time 10 minutes
Cook time 35 minutes

SERVES 8–12

This is an American cake that has become very popular. Some versions are quite dry, but this is lovely and moist. It is important to get the correct gel food colouring – it doesn't work with liquid cochineal colouring.

RED VELVET CAKE

- *2 cups sugar*
- *1 cup oil (soy, rice bran or canola)*
- *2 eggs*
- *1 cup buttermilk*
- *2 teaspoons vanilla*
- *2 tablespoons red gel food colouring*
- *2 teaspoons white vinegar*
- *2 teaspoons instant coffee powder, dissolved in ½ cup hot (not boiling) water*
- *2 cups flour*
- *1 teaspoon baking soda*
- *1 teaspoon baking powder*
- *1 teaspoon salt*
- *¼ cup cocoa*

Preheat the oven to 170°C. Spray two 22–23 cm spring-form tins with baking spray and line with baking paper.

In a large bowl, using an electric mixer, beat the sugar, oil and eggs together until pale and well combined. Add the buttermilk, vanilla, red gel colouring, vinegar and warm coffee.

Turn the mixer to low speed and add the dry ingredients, mixing until lightly combined. Divide between the prepared tins and bake for 35–40 minutes until a skewer inserted into the centre comes out clean.

Cool in the tins for 10–15 minutes, then carefully turn out onto a wire rack to cool completely.

When cold, sandwich the cakes together and frost with cream cheese frosting (see page 293).

Prep time 10 minutes
Cook time 40 minutes

SERVES 8–12

A great way to eat your vegetables. And a good way to use up a glut of zucchini in late summer. Grated zucchini (courgette) can be wrung out in a clean tea towel to remove excess water then frozen in zipped plastic bags. I measure it in 2-cup quantities, perfect to use for this recipe.

Walnut Zucchini Cake

- 125 G BUTTER, SOFTENED
- 1¾ CUPS SUGAR
- ½ CUP OIL (CANOLA, RICE BRAN, ETC.)
- 2 EGGS
- ½ CUP MILK
- 1 TEASPOON VANILLA
- ¼ CUP COCOA
- 2½ CUPS FLOUR
- 1 TEASPOON BAKING SODA
- 1 TEASPOON MIXED SPICE
- 2 CUPS WELL-SCRUBBED, GRATED ZUCCHINI

- 1 CUP CHOCOLATE CHIPS OR CHOPPED DARK CHOCOLATE PIECES
- ¾ CUP CHOPPED WALNUTS

For the frosting
- 4 CUPS ICING SUGAR
- ¼ CUP COCOA
- 125 G BUTTER, SOFTENED
- 250 G CREAM CHEESE, SOFTENED
- 1 TEASPOON VANILLA

Preheat the oven to 180°C. Spray two 23-cm spring-form cake tins with baking spray and line with baking paper.

Beat the butter and sugar together until creamy, then beat in the oil and eggs. Add the milk and vanilla, then stir in the sifted cocoa, flour, baking soda and spice. Fold in the grated zucchini, chocolate chips and walnuts. Pour the mixture into the prepared tins and bake for 25–30 minutes, until a skewer inserted into the middle of the cake comes out clean. Cool for 10 minutes in the tins, then carefully turn out and cool completely on a wire rack.

To make the frosting, sift the icing sugar and cocoa together, then add the remaining ingredients and beat until fluffy, smooth and well combined. Spread a third of the icing between the cakes and use the remainder to coat the top and sides of the cake. Keeps in an airtight container for up to a week.

Prep time 20 minutes
Cook time 30 minutes

SERVES 8-12

A fond childhood memory. The original recipe was a well-guarded secret of my Great Aunt Bea. It is written in her sister's (my Granny Win's) book as the 'best moist gingerbread – Bea's secret recipe'.

DARK MOIST GINGERBREAD

- 2 teaspoons mixed spice
- 1 teaspoon cinnamon
- 3 teaspoons ground ginger
- 2¼ cups flour
- 1 teaspoon baking powder
- 100 g butter
- 2 tablespoons golden syrup
- 1 tablespoon molasses
- ¾ cup brown sugar
- 1 cup milk
- 2 teaspoons baking soda
- ½ cup finely chopped crystallised ginger

Preheat the oven to 180°C. Spray a 10 x 20 x 7 cm loaf tin with baking spray and line with baking paper.

Place the spices, flour and baking powder in a bowl. Gently heat the butter, golden syrup, molasses and brown sugar. Stir until the butter is melted. Add the milk and then mix in the baking soda before stirring into the dry ingredients. Add the chopped ginger and mix really well. Pour into the prepared tin and bake for 35–40 minutes.

Cool in the tin for 10 minutes, then turn out onto a wire rack to cool completely. Serve in chunky slices. This is great served as a pudding with custard and cream or as an afternoon tea loaf. It is also good with cheese. It keeps very well. I usually wrap it in baking paper and keep it in an airtight container. Freezes well either as a loaf or in individual slices.

Prep time 15 minutes
Cook time 40 minutes

SERVES 8-12

A uniquely New Zealand cake. A feijoa is quite an individual taste and texture which I love. This is a good way to use up an excess crop and I've made it successfully with frozen feijoa pulp.

Feijoa Cake

- ½ CUP MILK
- 2 EGGS
- 1¼ CUPS SUGAR
- 1 CUP MASHED FEIJOAS (ABOUT 8 FEIJOAS)
- 1 TEASPOON VANILLA
- 75 G BUTTER, SOFTENED
- 2 CUPS FLOUR
- 1 TEASPOON BAKING POWDER
- 1 TEASPOON BAKING SODA
- ½ TEASPOON SALT

Preheat the oven to 180°C. Spray a 23-cm spring-form tin with baking spray and line with baking paper.

Place the milk, eggs, sugar, mashed feijoas, vanilla and butter in a food processor and process until smooth.

Place the dry ingredients in a bowl. Mix in the contents from the processor and combine well. Pour into the prepared tin and bake for 40–45 minutes until a skewer inserted into the centre comes out clean.

Cool for 5 minutes in the tin then remove and cool completely on a wire rack. Can be iced with lemon butter cream or fresh lemon icing (see page 290) and it is delicious dusted with icing sugar and served with thick yoghurt or softly whipped cream.

Prep time 10 minutes
Cook time 45 minutes

SERVES 8–12

HOSPICE CAKE

- 1 cup boiling water
- 1 cup chopped dried apricots (New Zealand apricots from Otago are my favourite)
- 200 g butter, softened
- ¾ cup sugar
- 3 eggs
- 1½ cups flour
- 1 teaspoon baking soda
- 1 teaspoon vanilla

FOR THE ICING

- approximately 2 cups icing sugar
- grated rind & juice of 1 orange
- 25 g butter, softened

Pour the boiling water over the apricots, then microwave for 5–7 minutes on high. Allow to cool for 20 minutes.

Preheat the oven to 180°C. Spray a 21–22 cm cake tin with baking spray and line the base with baking paper.

With an electric mixer, beat the butter and sugar together until light and fluffy. Add the eggs and flour. Stir the baking soda and vanilla into the cooled apricots and liquid, then add this to the flour mixture and combine well.

Pour into the prepared tin and bake for 45–50 minutes until a skewer inserted into the centre comes out clean.

Cool on a wire rack and ice when cold.

To make the icing, mix all the ingredients together until you have a smooth icing consistency. Spread over the cake, letting it drizzle down the sides.

Note: This cake works well in a ring tin but will take slightly less cooking time, about 35–40 minutes.

Prep time 15 minutes
Cook time 50 minutes

SERVES 10-12

I am a patron of Hospice New Zealand and one of the thousands of hospice volunteers around the country. I developed this cake to use for fundraising during Hospice Awareness Week. I know you will be making it more regularly, as it is so good and easy, and people request the recipe often. Feel free to make a donation to your local hospice any time you make the cake.

A big, quick and easy cake to feed people in a hurry. Equal ingredients mean it can be multiplied to fit larger tins, i.e. a big roasting tin is great for school camps or for feeding the workers morning tea. It can easily become a Coconut Lemon or Tangelo Drizzle Cake by substituting different citrus fruits.

Coconut Lime Drizzle Cake

- **2 CUPS COARSE THREAD COCONUT**
- **2 CUPS SELF-RAISING FLOUR**
- **2 CUPS SUGAR**
- **2 CUPS MILK (CAN BE LOW FAT)**
- **2 TEASPOONS VANILLA OR COCONUT ESSENCE**

For the topping
- **GRATED RIND & JUICE OF 3 LIMES**
- **1½ CUPS ICING SUGAR**

Preheat the oven to 180°C. Spray a 20 x 30 cm slice tin with baking spray and line with baking paper. Don't have too much overhang with the paper.

Mix the cake ingredients together in a bowl until well combined. Pour into the prepared tin and bake for 30 minutes. The golden-brown cake will be firm and pulling away from the sides of the tin. Remove from the oven and stand the tin on a wire rack to cool.

Mix the grated lime rind and juice and the icing sugar together to make a thin, runny icing. Drizzle this over the warm cake, spreading with a spatula.

Cool in the tin then set the icing in the fridge before cutting the cake into pieces. This is an excellent cake to serve warm with tropical fruit or strawberries as a dessert.

Tip: I have often iced this with chocolate icing, butter cream (see page 290), chocolate ganache (see page 293) or melted chocolate. When you top it with chocolate its chewy dense texture is like a Bounty Bar.

Prep time 5 minutes
Cook time 30 minutes

MAKES 20–25 PIECES

MRS BUTTON'S BILLY SPONGE

- *4 eggs*
- *1 cup sugar*
- *1 cup flour*
- *½ teaspoon baking powder*
- *extra ¼ cup sugar to sprinkle*

Preheat the oven to 180°C. Generously spray a 10 x 20 x 7 cm deep loaf tin with baking spray. Dust the tin with some extra sugar, shaking out any excess that doesn't stick to the surface.

With an electric mixer beat the eggs and sugar together until very thick and pale. Mix in the flour and baking powder and pour into the prepared tin. Sprinkle a little extra sugar over the top and bake for 30–35 minutes until well risen and rather cracked on the top.

Cool on a wire rack, then carefully ease out of the tin and slice when cold. The cake lasts 2–3 days stored in an airtight container and it makes a great dessert base topped with fruit and ice cream, or can be grilled or toasted. Individual slices can be frozen and they defrost quickly for impromptu coffee breaks or in sports bags or lunch boxes.

Prep time 5 minutes
Cook time 35 minutes

MAKES A LARGE LOAF

APPROX 20 SLICES

I have never discovered who Mrs Button was but she made a lovely billy sponge. This would obviously have been originally made in a billy suspended over a fire or in a coal range, but I've adapted it for a modern oven and non-stick loaf tin. Easy to make, simple ingredients and very delicious. Its smooth chewy texture is very moreish. I usually make this in a loaf tin but it works equally well in a small 20–21 cm round spring-form tin.

This is a really large, delicious citrus-flavoured cake. It makes a lovely cake-stand cake for a fancy afternoon tea. Get out the cake forks.

Whole Orange Cake

- 2 WHOLE ORANGES (SCRUBBED BUT NOT PEELED, AND ANY STICKERS REMOVED!)
- 400 G BUTTER, CUBED
- 6 EGGS
- 2 CUPS SUGAR
- 3 CUPS SELF-RAISING FLOUR

For the icing
- 3 CUPS ICING SUGAR
- 25 G BUTTER, MELTED
- GRATED RIND OF 1 ORANGE
- SQUEEZED JUICE OF THE ORANGE

Preheat the oven to 180°C. Spray a Bundt cake tin or alternatively an Angel Food Cake tin with baking spray and dust with flour. Shake out the excess flour.

Chop the oranges and remove any obvious pips. Place in a food processor and process until well puréed, then add the remaining ingredients and mix well. Pour into the prepared tin and bake for 45–55 minutes or until cooked. It may take less time (40–45 minutes) in an Angel Food Cake tin. Cool for 5 minutes in the tin then turn out onto a wire rack to cool completely.

To make the icing, mix the icing sugar, melted butter and grated orange rind with enough orange juice to make a smooth, pourable icing. Pour over the cake and allow to run down the sides.

This cake keeps well and can be made the day before. An easy dessert cake to serve with softly whipped cream or yoghurt and fruit.

Prep time 10 minutes
Cook time 55 minutes

SERVES 8–10

'Let's face it, a nice creamy chocolate cake does a lot for a lot of people. It does for me.'

Audrey Hepburn

One of our very popular café cakes. This tropical banana, pineapple and ginger cake is moist, and the cream cheese frosting never fails to please.

HUMMINGBIRD CAKE

- 3 cups flour
- 1 teaspoon baking soda
- 2 teaspoons ground ginger
- 1 cup sugar
- 1½ cups oil (soy, rice bran or canola)
- 3 eggs
- 1 x 225 g can crushed pineapple in juice, undrained
- 3 bananas, mashed
- 1 cup chopped blanched almonds
- 2 teaspoons vanilla
- ½ teaspoon salt

Preheat the oven to 180°C. Spray a 22–23 cm spring-form tin with baking spray and line the base with baking paper.

Mix all the ingredients in a food processor or an electric mixer until just combined. Pour into the prepared tin and bake for 1½ hours until golden brown. Leave in the tin for 15 minutes, then turn out and cool completely on a wire rack.

When cold, cut the cake into 2 or 3 layers and fill with cream cheese frosting (see page 293); spread this over the top and down the sides too. Allow the frosting to set before cutting. Best eaten in 3–4 days. Store in an airtight container in the fridge.

Tip: Use traditional cream cheese in the frosting but have it at room temperature. Lite and spreadable cream cheeses contain too much water and the result is gluey and too soft.

Prep time 15 minutes plus frosting
Cook time 1½ hours

SERVES 8–12

A quick, easy chocolate cake that is moist and delicious and tastes like an expensive chocolate truffle cake. The first chocolate cake I ever made and one of the most commonly grabbed-for recipes.

Basic Everyday Chocolate Cake

- 2 CUPS FLOUR
- ½ CUP COCOA
- 2 TEASPOONS BAKING POWDER
- 2 TEASPOONS BAKING SODA
- 2 CUPS CASTER SUGAR
- 1 CUP MILK, AT ROOM TEMPERATURE
- 1 CUP STRONG, WARM BLACK COFFEE
- 2 EGGS
- 100 G BUTTER, MELTED

Preheat the oven to 180°C. Spray a 23–24 cm spring-form tin with baking spray and line the base and sides with baking paper.

Sift the flour, cocoa, baking powder, baking soda and caster sugar into a large mixing bowl. In a separate bowl, mix the milk, coffee, eggs and melted butter together. Pour into the dry ingredients and mix well. Pour this quite runny mixture into the prepared tin and bake for 40–45 minutes until a skewer inserted into the centre comes out clean.

Cool for 10 minutes in the tin, then carefully release the sides and turn out to cool completely on a wire rack. When cold, ice with chocolate butter icing (see page 290) or pour over chocolate ganache (see page 293).

Prep time 15 minutes
Cook time 45 minutes

SERVES 10–12

A fabulous birthday cake for grown-ups. This is often requested by my girlfriends when we have a bit of a gals' evening. What better to serve with a round of long, icy cold gin & tonics – Seagers gin, of course.

GIN AND TONIC LEMON CAKE

- *200 g butter, softened*
- *1½ cups caster sugar*
- *grated rind of 2 lemons*
- *4 eggs*
- *2 cups flour*
- *2 teaspoons baking powder*
- *1 cup milk, at room temperature*

Preheat the oven to 180°C. Spray a 23–24 cm spring-form tin with baking spray and line the base and sides with baking paper.

In a large bowl, using an electric mixer, beat the butter and sugar together until pale and creamy. Add the lemon rind and the eggs, one at a time, beating well between each egg. Fold in the flour and baking powder along with the milk. Scrape into the prepared tin and bake for 45–55 minutes until the centre feels firm, the colour is golden brown and the cake has pulled away slightly from the sides of the tin.

Cool in the tin for 10 minutes, then carefully turn out onto a wire rack. Peel off the paper. Poke about 20–30 holes in the top of the cake using a skewer or toothpick. Drizzle over the gin and tonic syrup, allowing it to soak in before adding more. Use up all the syrup then cool the cake completely. Serve with whipped cream or lemon yoghurt.

Prep time 10 minutes
Cook time 55 minutes

SERVES 10-12

GIN AND TONIC SYRUP

- *½ cup gin*
- *¼ cup tonic water (can be diet – hahaha)*
- *1 cup sugar*
- *grated rind & juice of 1 lemon*

Place all the ingredients in a small saucepan and stir over low heat until the sugar is dissolved.

Bring to the boil once the sugar is dissolved. Pour the hot syrup over the warm cake.

Chocolate
is the
ANSWER.
Who cares what
the
question is.

This makes a good-sized rich chocolate log that can be filled with whipped cream or thick Greek-style yoghurt and fruit or with chocolate mousse and cream. At Christmas time I add a thin layer of Christmas mincemeat for a truly festive version.

Chocolate Roulade

- 5 EGGS, AT ROOM TEMPERATURE
- ¾ CUP CASTER SUGAR
- ¼ CUP SELF-RAISING FLOUR
- ¼ CUP COCOA
- ½ CUP GROUND ALMONDS

Preheat the oven to 200°C. Spray a 25 x 35 cm roulade or Swiss roll tin with baking spray and line with baking paper. Trim the paper to 1 cm above the sides of the tin. Spray the paper with baking spray.

In a large metal, china or glass bowl (not plastic) and using an electric mixer, beat the eggs and caster sugar together until pale, thick and ribbon-like. When you lift the beaters out of the mixture they should leave a ribbon trail on the surface. This will take 7–8 minutes, so don't be impatient.

Sift the flour, cocoa and ground almonds together, discarding any bits of coarse ground almond left behind. Fold the dry ingredients carefully and lightly into the egg mixture and then transfer into the prepared tin. Smooth the surface with a spatula. Bake for 10–12 minutes until the surface feels firm and springy and the roulade is pulling away from the sides of the tin.

Remove from the oven and carefully place a clean sheet of baking paper over the top of the roulade. Place a wire rack on top of the paper, then carefully turn over to remove from the tin. Peel the paper from the base. Roll lengthwise (from the long edge) using the clean sheet of paper to help you roll. Cool. Can be wrapped and frozen for 2–3 weeks.

When ready to fill, carefully unroll (defrosted first if frozen) and spread with whipped cream, raspberry jam, etc. as you desire. Re-roll. Dust generously with icing sugar, pour over warm chocolate ganache (see page 293) or ice with chocolate butter icing (see page 290).

Prep time 30 minutes
Cook time 12 minutes

SERVES 10–12

LEMON CURD *AND* WHIPPED CREAM SPONGE ROLL

- *4 eggs, at room temperature*
- *½ cup caster sugar*
- *½ cup self-raising flour*

FOR THE FILLING
- *300 ml cream*
- *1 cup lemon curd (see page 293)*
- *icing sugar, to dust*

Preheat the oven to 200°C. Spray a 25 x 35 cm Swiss roll or roulade tin with baking spray and line with baking paper. Trim the paper to 1 cm above the sides of the tin. Spray the paper with baking spray.

Wash a metal, glass or china (not plastic) bowl in boiling water to warm it. Dry well. Add the eggs and caster sugar and, with an electric mixer, beat them together until thick, pale and creamy. It should be thick enough so that when you lift the beaters out of the mixture they will leave ribbons across the surface. Do not be impatient with this step; it will take 6–8 minutes of beating.

Sift the flour and carefully fold into the egg mixture. Spread into the prepared tin and smooth the surface with a spatula. Bake for 7–8 minutes until pale golden brown, well risen and pulling away from the sides of the tin.

Remove from the oven. Lay a clean sheet of baking paper over the top of the sponge and then a wire cooling rack over this. Carefully flip over then lift off the tin. Carefully peel off the baking paper and cool completely.

Whip the cream to the desired thickness and keep chilled as the sponge cools. Minimum cooling time will be 15–20 minutes.

Lightly score a line along one of the long edges of the sponge, about 1 cm from the edge. This helps with the first roll.

Using a spatula or palette knife, evenly spread the lemon curd over the sponge, right to the edges. Add a layer of whipped cream, also spreading to the edges. Roll towards you, starting with the scored edge side. Use the paper to keep the roll tight and round like a sushi roll. Transfer to a serving platter and dust with icing sugar. Serve with extra whipped cream if desired. Slice with a serrated knife, wiping after each creamy slice.

Handy tip: For a dessert version, I replace the whipped cream with softened ice-cream and keep it in the freezer. The result is known as an Arctic Roll.

Prep time 30 minutes
Cook time 8 minutes

SERVES 8-12

Sponge rolls are very impressive but actually darn easy to make. This one never fails to win me brownie points and is a frequent 'go to' recipe when, for whatever reason, I need a cake in a hurry. This one is filled with a delicious combination of sharp, tart lemon curd and whipped cream, but it could be any jam, or spread with yoghurt for equally praiseworthy 'raves'.

Claudia is photographer Jae Frew's daughter and my fairy god-daughter. She has been helping with my cookbooks and baking for years. She started out as one of the featured children in earlier cookbook photographs, with her little child's hands holding raspberries or a cupcake. She always helps on our photography shoots and is a star in the kitchen. This lovely Rosewater Cake is her favourite thing to make and is affectionately known to us as Claudia's Truffle Ruffle Cake.

Claudia's Rosewater Cake

- 250 G BUTTER, SOFTENED
- 1¾ CUPS CASTER SUGAR
- 3 EGGS
- 2¾ CUPS FLOUR
- 4 TEASPOONS BAKING POWDER
- ½ TEASPOON SALT
- 1¼ CUPS MILK
- 1 TABLESPOON ROSEWATER

For the rosewater butter cream frosting

- 225 G BUTTER, SOFTENED
- 5 CUPS ICING SUGAR
- 100 ML MILK
- 1 TEASPOON VANILLA
- A FEW DROPS PINK FOOD COLOURING
- 1 TABLESPOON ROSEWATER

Preheat the oven to 150°C. Spray the bases and sides of two 18 cm cake tins with baking spray and line with baking paper.

Beat the butter and caster sugar together with an electric mixer until light, pale and fluffy. Add the eggs one at a time, beating well between each addition. Add the dry ingredients, milk and rosewater, mixing on low speed and scraping down the bowl as it mixes. The mixture needs to be well combined but not overworked.

Pour into the prepared tins and smooth the surface level with a spatula. Bake for 40–45 minutes until the surface springs back when pressed in the centre and a skewer comes out clean. Cool in the tins for 10 minutes, then carefully turn out onto a wire rack to cool completely.

Place one cake on top of the other, sandwiching them together with frosting mixture before frosting the sides and top of the cake.

To make the frosting

Beat the butter and 2 cups of icing sugar together until very pale and fluffy. Add the milk, vanilla, food colouring and rosewater then beat in the remainder of the icing sugar half a cup at a time until the frosting is the desired consistency for easy piping.

You may not need to use all the icing sugar.

Spoon into a piping bag fitted with a flat 1 cm star tip. Pipe out in rosette shapes as illustrated, covering the whole outer surfaces of the cake. Allow to set before carefully transferring to a cake stand or cake serving plate.

Tips for frosting the rosette pattern

Using a palette knife, spread icing all over the sides and top of the cake. Then start by piping the rosette shapes at the bottom of the cake, 4 cm up from the base. This will be the centre of the rosette. Go right around the base, then make the second row 4 cm up from the first rosette. In a circular motion, start at the centre of each rosette and then spread outwards so they touch each other, filling the gaps. Be quite firm with the piping so that the frosting really presses into the cake surface. Repeat the rows until the entire cake is covered. Allow the frosting to firm and set for at least 2 hours before cutting.

Makes a small but quite high 18 cm cake
Prep time 15 minutes
Cook time 45 minutes
Icing time 45 minutes

SERVES 8-10

MUFFINS, SCONES AND LOAVES

This is my own adaptation of traditional scones. The butter is melted in the warm milk, then mixed with the self-raising flour, activating the raising agent quickly. I find it a very successful method without having to rub the butter into the flour first. We use it in the café and get some lovely comments about our scones.

FARMHOUSE SCONES

- *3 cups self-raising flour*
- *½ teaspoon salt*
- *50 g butter*
- *approximately 1 cup milk*

Preheat the oven to 220°C. Spray a baking tray with baking spray.

Place the flour and salt in a large bowl. Stir the butter and milk over gentle heat, or microwave until the butter melts. Pour into the flour and mix to a soft dough, adding extra milk (cold) if required. Very gently knead (don't over-handle) the dough and press flat to 3 cm thick.

Cut out squares or rounds and place on the prepared tray. Brush with milk and bake for 15–20 minutes until golden brown. Cool on the tray. Cover with a clean tea towel to keep the scones soft and moist. These keep well. Can be microwaved for a few seconds to refresh.

Prep time 5 minutes
Cook time 20 minutes

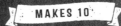

MAKES 10

Lots of variations are possible –

- ADD CHOPPED DATES AND ¼ CUP CASTER SUGAR
- ADD RAISINS OR SULTANAS AND ¼ CUP CASTER SUGAR
- FOR CHEESE SCONES, ADD A HANDFUL OF GRATED TASTY CHEESE TO THE DOUGH WITH ½ TEASPOON DRIED MUSTARD POWDER OR GARLIC SALT. A LITTLE SPRINKLE OF CHEESE ON THE TOP IS NICE TOO.

TIP: IF YOU PREFER SOFT EDGES ON YOUR SCONES, KEEP THEM CLOSE TOGETHER ON THE BAKING TRAY SO THEY JUST TOUCH AT THE SIDES.

My version of Lemonade Scones. I think the Lemon & Paeroa gives it a nice New Zealand flavour.

Lemon & Paeroa Scones

- 4 CUPS SELF-RAISING FLOUR
- 300 ML CREAM
- 1 X 355 ML CAN LEMON & PAEROA
- ½ TEASPOON SALT

Preheat the oven to 220°C. Spray a baking tray with baking spray.

Mix all the ingredients in a bowl to a smooth dough. Tip out onto a well-floured bench and cut into squares or press out with a round cookie cutter. Place on the prepared tray, close together. Bake for 15–20 minutes until starting to colour golden. Check they are cooked through and cool on a wire rack.

Tip: Brushing with milk before baking will add a good golden colouring if desired.

Prep time 5 minutes
Cook time 20 minutes

MAKES 10-12

The 'cream tea' tradition of fresh scones spread with jam and clotted or whipped cream is fairly synonymous with the counties of Devon and Cornwall in the south of England, but is eaten as a special treat all over the world these days.

It has always been associated with rather a fancy high tea occasion in my family. Certainly a popular afternoon tea treat in the café at the weekend. As children we ate scones like this as an impromptu dessert.

You can see my grandsons tucking in – the family tradition continues.

This is my take on the Chelsea Bun. The original is from the famous 'Chelsea Bun Shop' in Chelsea, London. We've innovated a little but I think they are great, and they're a very popular item in the café. We always serve them slightly warmed.

Chelsea Buns

For the dough
- 4 CUPS SELF-RAISING FLOUR
- 100 G COLD BUTTER, CUT INTO SMALL CUBES
- ¼ CUP CASTER SUGAR
- ½ TEASPOON SALT
- 1½ CUPS MILK

For the filling
- 60 G BUTTER, SOFTENED TO ROOM TEMPERATURE
- ½ CUP BROWN SUGAR
- 1 TEASPOON CINNAMON
- 1½ CUPS MIXED DRIED FRUIT (RAISINS, CURRANTS, SULTANAS, ETC.)

For the glaze
- 1 TABLESPOON APRICOT JAM
- 1 TABLESPOON WATER

For the icing
- 1 CUP ICING SUGAR

Preheat the oven to 180°C. Line a 25 x 35 cm sponge-roll tin or medium-sized roasting tin with baking paper.

In a large bowl, place the flour, cubes of butter, caster sugar and salt. Using your fingertips, rub the butter into the dry ingredients. Using a spatula or metal spoon, mix in the milk to form a soft dough.

Generously sprinkle flour onto a board or bench surface and turn out the dough. Pat or gently roll out the dough into a rectangle about 1 cm thick.

To make the filling, beat the butter, brown sugar and cinnamon together in a small bowl, mixing until smoothly combined. Spread this over the dough like buttering toast and then sprinkle with the dried fruit.

Roll the dough up from the long side into a log. Cut into 14 slices. Place side by side in the prepared tin. Bake for 20–25 minutes until risen and lightly golden brown.

Warm the apricot jam and water (can be done in the microwave) and mix until smooth. Brush over the warm buns and allow to cool in the tin.

Mix the icing sugar with enough water to make a thin, pourable icing. Place the icing in a small squeezy bottle and, when the glaze has dried, drizzle lines of icing over the buns and dust with icing sugar. When the buns are cool and the icing set, serve. They are delicious served warm.

Prep time 20 minutes
Cook time 25 minutes

MAKES 14

HOT CROSS BUNS

FOR THE DOUGH

- 2 tablespoons dried yeast granules (15 g or 2 sachets)
- 1 cup warm water
- 2 teaspoons caster sugar
- 7 cups flour (use high-grade or bread-making flour)
- 1 teaspoon salt
- extra ½ cup caster sugar
- ¾ cup raisins or sultanas
- ¾ cup currants
- ½ cup mixed peel
- 2 tablespoons cinnamon
- 2 tablespoons mixed spice
- 2 cups milk, warmed
- 75 g butter, melted
- 1 egg, lightly beaten

FOR THE CROSSES

- ¾ cup flour
- ¼ cup water (approximately)

FOR THE GLAZE

- ¼ cup caster sugar
- 2 tablespoons hot water

Spray a large sponge-roll tin or roasting dish with baking spray.

In a large bowl, mix the yeast, warm water and 2 teaspoons of caster sugar. Leave until it becomes active and frothy, about 10–15 minutes. Add all the other dough ingredients, kneading together well to form a smooth dough. I use my electric mixer with a dough hook for this. Spray a large bowl with oil and place the dough in this. Cover with a clean tea towel or cling film. Place the bowl in a warm, draught-free area like a sunny windowsill or the warming cupboard.

When the dough has doubled in size (approximately 1 hour) punch it down and knead for 5–6 minutes. Divide the dough into 24 pieces and place side by side in the prepared tin. Cover and rest in the warm place again for a further 30 minutes to rise.

Preheat the oven to 200°C.

Mix the flour and water for the crosses into a thick paste. Using a piping bag or small plastic bag with one corner cut out, pipe crosses on the top of each bun. Bake for 20–25 minutes until medium golden brown, well risen and cooked through. Remove from the oven and cool the tin on a wire rack.

Mix the sugar and hot water together for the glaze until the sugar has dissolved. Brush over the buns while they are still warm. Cool completely. Carefully remove from the tray and pull the buns apart. Re-warm and serve with lashings of butter.

Prep time 20 minutes
Rest time 1½ hours
Cook time 25 minutes

MAKES 24

HOMEMADE HOT CROSS BUNS ARE EXCEPTIONALLY GOOD AND WE USE THIS RECIPE TO MAKE DOZENS EACH YEAR IN THE CAFÉ.

A delicious banana loaf particularly loved by children. This keeps well if wrapped in tinfoil or cling film and freezes marvellously. I slice it into thick slabs and individually freeze these in small ziplock bags which can be tossed into a lunch box or tucked into a ski jacket or the rugby bag. For a special treat you can add chunks of chocolate or chocolate chips – about half a cup.

Banana Pecan Bread

- 1¾ CUPS FLOUR
- 1 TEASPOON BAKING SODA
- ½ TEASPOON SALT
- 5 VERY RIPE BANANAS, WELL MASHED
- 125 G BUTTER, MELTED
- 2 EGGS
- ¾ CUP BROWN SUGAR
- 1 TEASPOON VANILLA
- ½ CUP PECAN PIECES OR CHOPPED WHOLE PECANS

Preheat the oven to 180°C. Line a large 22 x 12 x 7 cm deep loaf tin with baking paper.

Mix all the ingredients together in a large bowl until well combined. Do not overmix. Scrape into the prepared tin and bake for 45–50 minutes until golden brown and a skewer inserted into the centre comes out clean. The loaf will have pulled away from the sides of the tin.

Cool in the tin for 15 minutes, then carefully turn out onto a wire rack, peel off the paper and cool completely. Slice when cold.

This loaf is quite moist so I don't usually have it buttered. Keep it well wrapped in tinfoil or cling film for 4–5 days. Can be frozen.

Prep time 5 minutes
Cook time 50 minutes

MAKES 14–15 THICK SLICES

DATE AND WALNUT LOAF

- *1 cup pitted dates, coarsely chopped*
- *1 teaspoon baking soda*
- *1 cup boiling water or hot black tea*
- *1 cup brown sugar*
- *1 egg*
- *1 tablespoon butter, melted*
- *1 teaspoon vanilla*
- *2 cups self-raising flour*
- *½ cup walnut pieces*

Place the dates in a bowl with the baking soda and hot water or tea. Set aside for half an hour for the dates to soften.

Preheat the oven to 160°C. Line a 20 x 10 x 7 cm deep loaf tin with baking paper.

Mix the brown sugar, egg, melted butter and vanilla together with the softened dates, including the liquid. Mix in the flour and walnuts.

Pour into the prepared tin and bake for approximately 1 hour, until dark golden brown and a skewer inserted into the centre comes out clean.

Cool in the tin for 15 minutes, then carefully lift out, peel off the paper, and cool on a wire rack.

Prep time 35 minutes
Cook time 1 hour

MAKES 1 LOAF

THIS LOAF IS WONDERFUL SLICED AND BUTTERED. PERFECT FOR MORNING TEA OR IN LUNCH BOXES.

I make this with trim milk and it is almost fat free. It is always popular. It is easy to slice even from frozen and delicious served warm with butter. At Christmas time I've used dried fruit with red and green cherries in it for a sneaky quick Christmas loaf.

HEALTHY SULTANA BRAN LOAF

- 2 cups raw sugar
- 2 cups bran flakes (baking bran)
- 2 cups sultanas or mixed dried fruit
- 2 cups milk (can be low fat)
- 2 cups self-raising flour

Preheat the oven to 150°C. Line a 22 x 12 x 7 cm tin with baking paper.

Mix all the ingredients together and scrape into the prepared tin. Bake for 1¼–1½ hours until golden and firm when pressed in the centre. Cool in the tin, then turn out onto a wire rack. Slice and serve either buttered or plain.

This keeps very well and stays moist. It can be toasted or a slice cut into little squares to serve with cheese. Particularly good with blue cheese. It can also be thinly sliced and dried in the oven like a biscotti, which is lovely on a cheeseboard.

Note: I have made this into really large loaves or even a square cake for shearing gangs, school camps, etc. It is equal quantities of all five ingredients whether you use an empty yoghurt pot or a plastic bucket – so long as you use the same measure and adjust the cooking time it works well.

Prep time 5 minutes
Cook time 1½ hours

MAKES 1 LOAF

LOVELY TO SLICE AND BUTTER.
THIS LOAF KEEPS WELL AND CAN
BE FROZEN TOO.

Apricot & Walnut Tea Loaf

- 125 G BUTTER, SOFTENED TO ROOM TEMPERATURE
- ½ CUP BROWN SUGAR
- ¼ CUP (4 TABLESPOONS) GOLDEN SYRUP
- ¾ CUP BUTTERMILK
- 1 TABLESPOON GRATED ORANGE RIND
- 1½ CUPS SELF-RAISING FLOUR
- 2 TEASPOONS MIXED SPICE
- 2 EGGS
- ½ CUP CHOPPED WALNUTS
- 1 CUP CHOPPED DRIED APRICOTS (NEW ZEALAND DRIED APRICOTS FROM OTAGO ARE THE BEST FLAVOUR FOR THIS LOAF)

Preheat the oven to 180°C. Line a 20 x 10 x 7 cm deep loaf tin with baking paper.

Beat the butter, brown sugar and golden syrup together until creamy and smooth. Add the remaining ingredients and mix well. Scrape into the prepared tin and bake for 55–60 minutes until deep golden brown and firm when pressed in the centre.

Cool in the tin for 10 minutes then turn out onto a wire rack to cool completely. Slice when cold and butter if desired.

This loaf keeps well wrapped in tinfoil or cling film. Freezes well.

Tip: You can measure out buttermilk and freeze in small plastic ziplock bags or containers. It is handy if you write the measure on the side, i.e. ¾ cup, for future reference.

Prep time 15 minutes
Cook time 1 hour

MAKES 14–16 SLICES

Drizzle is not always such a good word when related to the weather, i.e. falling from the sky, but this super-easy loaf is always a welcome treat. It gets lots of brownie points and is, in my opinion, the perfect accompaniment to a cup of tea.

LEMON DRIZZLE LOAF

- *175 g butter, softened to room temperature*
- *¾ cup caster sugar*
- *2 lemons*
- *¼ teaspoon salt*
- *3 eggs*
- *¾ cup self-raising flour*
- *¾ cup ground almonds*
- *¼ cup milk*
- *½ cup sugar*

Preheat the oven to 180°C. Line a 20 x 10 x 7 cm deep loaf tin with baking paper.

Beat the butter and caster sugar together until light and fluffy. Add the grated rind of 1 lemon. Add the salt and eggs, one at a time, beating well after each addition. Mix in the flour, ground almonds and milk. When well combined, scrape into the prepared tin and bake for 55–60 minutes until well risen (it may crack a little) and a skewer inserted in the centre comes out clean.

Mix together the grated rind of the remaining lemon and the squeezed juice of both lemons along with the sugar.

Using the testing skewer, poke about 20 holes into the loaf then drizzle over the sugar and lemon mixture. Allow time for the drizzle to soak into the warm cake, absorbing the liquid, before you add more.

Cool in the tin then carefully remove to a wire rack. Keeps for 3–4 days well wrapped in tinfoil or cling film. Freezes well.

Prep time 10 minutes
Cook time 1 hour

SERVES 10-12

In my kitchen I'm preheating memories, folding in old friends and new, and baking a good laugh.

A FAVOURITE CAFÉ MUFFIN AND IT IS HARD TO STOP AT ONE. THESE CAN BE SERVED WARM AS A DESSERT WITH ICE CREAM OR YOGHURT AND FRESH BERRIES.

Raspberry White Chocolate Muffins

- 2 CUPS FLOUR
- ¾ CUP SUGAR
- 4 TEASPOONS BAKING POWDER
- 1 EGG
- ¼ CUP OIL OR 100 G BUTTER, MELTED
- 1 CUP MILK
- 1 TEASPOON RASPBERRY ESSENCE
- 1 CUP RASPBERRIES (CAN USE FROZEN BERRIES BUT KEEP FROZEN, DO NOT DEFROST FIRST)
- ¾ CUP CHOPPED WHITE CHOCOLATE (OR WHITE CHOCOLATE BITS OR BUTTONS)

Preheat the oven to 200°C. Spray a 12-cup muffin tin with baking spray and, if desired, line with paper cases.

Mix all the ingredients together in a large bowl until just combined. Do not overwork the mixture or the muffins will lose their lightness. Spoon into the prepared tins and bake for 15–18 minutes. They will be well risen and golden brown.

These are great dusted with icing sugar before serving.

Prep time 10 minutes
Cook time 18 minutes

MAKES 12
REGULAR-SIZED MUFFINS

PEACHES AND CREAM CHEESE MUFFINS

- 2 cups flour
- ¾ cup sugar
- 4 teaspoons baking powder
- 1 egg
- ¼ cup oil or 100 g butter, melted
- 1 cup milk
- 1 cup chopped fresh (or drained canned) peaches
- 1 teaspoon vanilla
- 125 g cream cheese (the firm traditional style is best)

Preheat the oven to 200°C. Spray a 12-cup muffin tin with baking spray and, if desired, line with paper cases.

Mix all the ingredients, except the cream cheese, together in a large bowl until just combined. Do not overwork the mixture or the muffins will lose their lightness. Spoon into the prepared tins. Cut the cream cheese into 12 equal-sized cubes or pieces. Poke one piece of cream cheese into each muffin.

Bake for 15–18 minutes. They will be well risen and golden brown.

These are great dusted with icing sugar before serving.

Prep time 10 minutes
Cook time 18 minutes

MAKES 12
REGULAR-SIZED MUFFINS

THESE ARE ONE OF MY FAVOURITE COMBINATIONS – NOT OVERLY SWEET AND VERY MOIST.

Of course these can be made with dark or white chocolate, but the milk chocolate version was always my children's favourite and my daughter Kate now makes these to the delight of her two wee boys.

Chocolate

Chocolate

5501

Banana Milk Chocolate Muffins

- 2 CUPS FLOUR
- ¾ CUP SUGAR
- 4 TEASPOONS BAKING POWDER
- 1 EGG
- ¼ CUP OIL OR 100 G BUTTER, MELTED
- 1 CUP MILK
- 2–3 BANANAS, MASHED WITH A FORK TO MAKE 1 CUPFUL
- 1 TEASPOON VANILLA
- ¾ CUP CHOPPED MILK CHOCOLATE (OR MILK CHOCOLATE BITS OR BUTTONS)

Preheat the oven to 200°C. Spray a 12-cup muffin tin with baking spray and, if desired, line with paper cases.

Mix all the ingredients together in a large bowl until just combined. Do not overwork the mixture or the muffins will lose their lightness. Spoon into the prepared tins. Bake for 15–18 minutes. They will be well risen and golden brown.

These are great dusted with icing sugar before serving.

Prep time 10 minutes
Cook time 18 minutes

MAKES 12
REGULAR-SIZED MUFFINS

These are lovely served warm with lemon curd and dusted with icing sugar. A real teatime treat.

BLUEBERRY LEMON MUFFINS

- 2¼ cups flour
- ¾ cup caster sugar
- 4 teaspoons baking powder
- 1 egg
- ¼ cup oil or 100 g butter, melted
- 1 cup milk
- grated rind of 2 lemons
- ¼ cup fresh lemon juice
- 1 cup blueberries (can be frozen, but do not thaw)

Preheat the oven to 200°C. Spray a 12-cup muffin tin with baking spray and, if desired, line with paper cases.

Mix all the ingredients together in a large bowl until just combined. Do not overwork the mixture or the muffins will lose their lightness. Spoon into the prepared tins.

Bake for 15–18 minutes. They will be well risen and golden brown. Dust with icing sugar to serve.

Prep time 10 minutes
Cook time 18 minutes

MAKES 12
REGULAR-SIZED MUFFINS

The dried mustard powder really is the secret to these moreish savoury cheese muffins.

Savoury Cheese & Bacon Muffins

- 2 CUPS FLOUR
- 4 TEASPOONS BAKING POWDER
- 1 EGG
- ¼ CUP OIL OR 100 G BUTTER, MELTED
- 1 CUP MILK
- 1 CUP GRATED TASTY CHEESE
- 2–3 RASHERS LEAN BACON, SNIPPED OR CHOPPED INTO LITTLE 2 CM PIECES
- 1 SPRING ONION, FINELY CHOPPED
- ½ TEASPOON GARLIC SALT
- ½ TEASPOON FRESHLY GROUND BLACK PEPPER
- 1 TEASPOON DRIED MUSTARD POWDER

Preheat the oven to 200°C. Spray a 12-cup muffin tin with baking spray and, if desired, line with paper cases.

Mix all the ingredients together in a large bowl until just combined. Do not overwork the mixture or the muffins will lose their lightness. Spoon into the prepared tins.

Bake for 15–18 minutes. They will be well risen and golden brown.

Prep time 10 minutes
Cook time 18 minutes

MAKES 12
REGULAR-SIZED MUFFINS

These are literally a perfect breakfast to eat as you run for a bus or on the way to school in a hurry. Great in a lunch box too.

BREAKFAST ON THE RUN, FRUITY BRAN MUFFINS

- *1½ cups flour*
- *2 teaspoons baking powder*
- *1½ cups bran flakes (baking bran)*
- *½ cup brown sugar*
- *¾ cup mixed dried fruit (sultanas, chopped dates, etc.)*
- *2 tablespoons golden syrup*
- *50 g butter*
- *1 teaspoon baking soda*
- *1 cup milk*
- *1 egg*

Preheat the oven to 200°C. Spray a 12-cup muffin tin with baking spray and, if desired, line with paper cases.

In a large bowl, mix the flour, baking powder, bran, brown sugar and dried fruit together. In a small saucepan or microwave bowl, heat the golden syrup and butter together, stirring until the butter has melted. Mix the baking soda with the milk and egg, then mix everything together, folding just enough to combine. Do not overwork the mixture.

Spoon into the prepared tins and bake for 12–15 minutes until springy when pressed in the centre. Cool in the tin for 5 minutes, then carefully turn out onto a wire rack. If desired, serve buttered.

Prep time 10 minutes
Cook time 15 minutes

MAKES 12
REGULAR-SIZED MUFFINS

AFTERNOON TEA
AND FANCY CAKES

The first time these appeared in a published cookbook was in 1951, in the League of Mothers collection of recipes. They were attributed to Mrs Brown of South Dunedin. The 'oyster' part of the name may have been a clue to the shape of the little cakes, split with cream between the halves, making them look a little like an oyster. Or perhaps Mrs Brown lived near New Zealand's famous Bluff oyster beds. Who knows? They are a favourite of mine.

CINNAMON OYSTERS

TO PREPARE THE TINS
- 3 tablespoons caster sugar
- 3 tablespoons flour

FOR THE OYSTERS
- 3 eggs
- ¼ cup caster sugar
- 1 tablespoon golden syrup, warmed
- 6 tablespoons flour
- 1 teaspoon cinnamon
- ½ teaspoon baking soda
- 1 teaspoon ground ginger
- freshly whipped cream, to fill
- icing sugar, to dust

Preheat the oven to 180°C. Mix the caster sugar and flour together. Spray a tray of shallow 'patty pans' (or use shallow tart tins) with baking spray, then dust with the sugar/flour mixture. Shake out any excess. I find shaking it out onto a sheet of paper then reusing the excess works well.

Beat the eggs and second measure of caster sugar together with an electric mixer until pale and fluffy. Add the warmed golden syrup and beat really well to a thick ribbony consistency. Sift in the dry ingredients, then carefully fold into the mixture. Spoon into the prepared tins, filling about three-quarters full.

Bake for 7–10 minutes until puffed up and deep golden brown. Turn out onto a wire rack to cool and continue with a second batch until the mixture is used up.

When completely cool, use a small serrated knife to split each cake almost in half like a bread roll. Fill with whipped cream and dust with icing sugar to serve. Best eaten on the day they are baked.

Prep time 30 minutes
Cook time 10 minutes

MAKES 30–32

Everybody loves brownies but this is special, a little bite-size format with fudgy frosting. The perfect size treat. Easy to make, these have become my modern version for a 'bring a plate' occasion. They can be customised for Easter by topping with a little Easter egg or bunny, for Christmas with a candy cane or festive sweeties, and with flowers or fairies or pirates etc. for birthday celebrations.

Fudge Brownie Bites

- 150 G DARK CHOCOLATE (72% COCOA SOLIDS IS BEST)
- 150 G BUTTER
- 3 EGGS
- 1 CUP CASTER SUGAR
- ¾ CUP FLOUR
- ¼ CUP COCOA
- 1 TEASPOON VANILLA

Preheat the oven to 170°C. Spray a 24-cup mini-muffin tray with baking spray.

Melt the chocolate and butter together in the microwave on medium, stirring after every 20-second burst, until smoothly combined.

Beat the eggs and sugar together until thick and pale. Mix in the melted chocolate, then sift in the flour and cocoa and add the vanilla. Mix until well combined.

Spoon into the prepared muffin tin and bake for 18–20 minutes until just firm and set. Cool for 3 minutes in the tin then turn out carefully onto a wire rack. Wait until they are completely cold before frosting. These freeze well unfrosted.

Prep time 10 minutes plus decorating
Cook time 20 minutes

MAKES 24

Frosting

- 100 G BUTTER, SOFTENED
- ½ TEASPOON VANILLA
- 3 CUPS ICING SUGAR
- ½ CUP COCOA
- BOILING WATER TO MIX

Using an electric mixer, beat the butter, vanilla and icing sugar together. Add the sifted cocoa and enough boiling water to make a smooth, spreadable consistency.

Spread or pipe onto the brownie bites and garnish as desired. Once frosted, store in an airtight container for up to 4 days.

ORANGE MADELEINES

- 2 tablespoons golden syrup
- 100 g butter, melted
- 2 eggs
- ¼ cup caster sugar
- ½ cup flour
- 1 teaspoon grated orange rind
- 1 teaspoon baking powder
- icing sugar, to dust

Preheat the oven to 170°C. Spray a Madeleine mould with baking spray and dust with flour, shaking off the excess.

Stir the golden syrup into the melted butter and cool. Beat the eggs and caster sugar together until pale and fluffy. Gently mix the flour, orange rind, baking powder and the golden syrup mixture into the beaten eggs.

Spoon into the prepared mould, filling to only three-quarters full, then bake for 7–10 minutes. Cool on a wire rack and dust with icing sugar to serve. Best eaten the day they are made.

Prep time 10 minutes
Cook time 10 minutes

MAKES 18-24

DEPENDING ON SIZE OF MOULDS

THIS RECIPE IS BASED ON A CLASSIC
FRIAND RECIPE AND IS EASILY
ADAPTED TO BE GLUTEN FREE.

Raspberry & Almond High Tea Cakes

- 175 G BUTTER, MELTED
- 1 CUP GROUND ALMONDS
- 1¼ CUPS ICING SUGAR
- ½ CUP FLOUR (OR GLUTEN-FREE FLOUR MIX)
- 5 EGG WHITES
- 24 RASPBERRIES (FRESH OR FROZEN)
- ½ CUP FLAKED ALMONDS
- ICING SUGAR, TO DUST

Preheat the oven to 180°C. Spray a 24-cup mini-muffin tin with baking spray. Silicone trays work well for this recipe.

Make sure the melted butter has cooled.

Place the ground almonds, icing sugar and flour in a mixing bowl. Add the unbeaten egg whites and the cooled melted butter. Mix well – an electric mixer is great for this.

Spoon about 2 teaspoons of mixture into each muffin cup. Place a raspberry in each by poking them in the top of the mixture. Sprinkle a few flaked almonds over. Bake for 12–15 minutes. Cool for 5 minutes in the tin, then carefully remove and cool completely on a wire rack. Dust with icing sugar to serve.

This mixture can be made ahead and stored in the fridge for 4–5 days. It thickens on cooling and may take a minute or two longer to cook if the mixture is cold.

Note: Make sure the melted butter has cooled down before adding it to the raw egg whites, otherwise the heat will cook the egg whites like scrambled eggs.

Best eaten the day they are baked, although the unbaked mixture keeps well in the fridge.

Prep time 10 minutes
Cook time 15 minutes

MAKES 24
MINI-MUFFIN-SIZED DAINTIES

These are just the best. Crisp, vanilla flavoured, with a good gooey chewy centre. A recipe I have been making forever and one that is frequently requested. The mixture can be piped for perfect meringues or dolloped out for a more free-range look.

PERFECT MERINGUES

- *6 egg whites, at room temperature*
- *2 cups caster sugar*
- *1 teaspoon vanilla*
- *1 teaspoon vinegar*
- *2 teaspoons cornflour*
- *whipped cream, to serve*

Preheat the oven to 120°C. Line a baking tray with baking paper.

In a large metal, porcelain or glass (not plastic) bowl, beat the egg whites until soft peaks form. Gradually, a teaspoon at a time, add the caster sugar. The mixture should be getting glossy, thick and shiny with each addition and the whole sugar-adding process should take at least 10 minutes. Beat in the vanilla, vinegar and cornflour.

Spoon the mixture into blobs or pipe out onto the prepared tray.

Bake for approximately 45 minutes until dry and crisp. The meringues should lift off the paper easily. Cool on a wire rack and sandwich together with whipped cream when cold.

Unfilled meringues keep well in an airtight container for 3–4 days.

Prep time 15 minutes
Cook time 45 minutes

MAKES 36-40

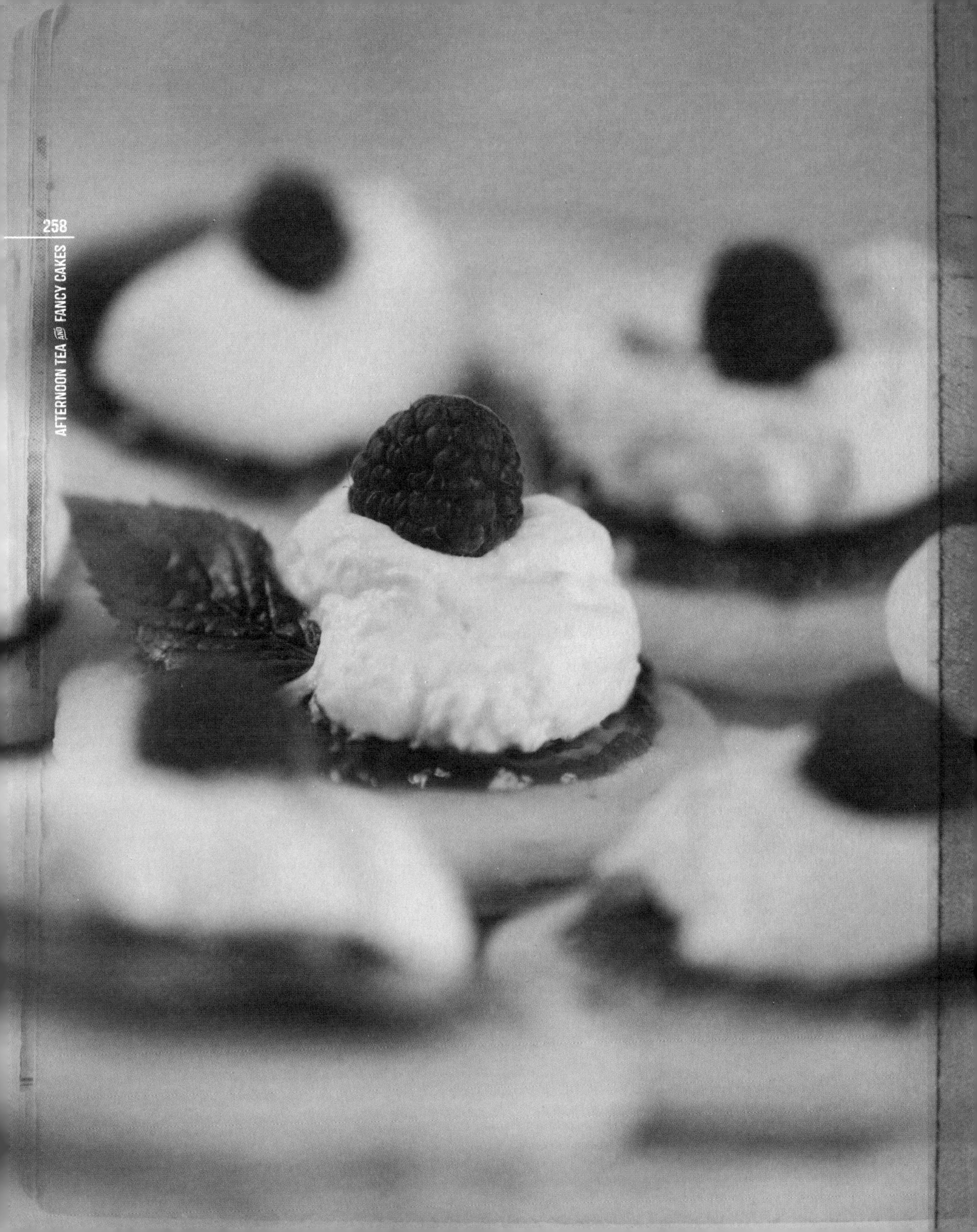

These are incredibly easy to make and seem such a perfect afternoon tea treat. When we were children we used to make them for Dad after he mowed the lawns in the weekend. We always had raspberry jam on them, but whipped cream was only for special occasions, like a birthday. This recipe makes nice thick pikelets that aren't all bendy and floppy when you eat them. The secret is using cream of tartar and baking soda rather than commercial baking powder.

Pikelets

- 1 TEASPOON BAKING SODA
- 1¼ CUPS MILK
- 1 EGG
- 3 TABLESPOONS SUGAR
- 2 CUPS FLOUR
- 2 TEASPOONS CREAM OF TARTAR

To serve
- FRUIT JAM
- WHIPPED CREAM OR THICK YOGHURT
- FRUIT TO GARNISH

Dissolve the baking soda in the milk.

Beat the egg and sugar together, then mix in the flour and cream of tartar. Add in the milk and baking soda mixture and mix to a smooth batter, using a little extra milk if required. I use a blender for mixing the batter. Spoon onto a heated non-stick or well-greased heavy frypan or crêpe pan.

When making pikelets, if you drop the mixture off the end of the spoon they will be uniformly round. Spooning into the pan from the side of a spoon makes oval and misshapen pikelets.

Cook over medium heat until bubbles appear and the surface is golden brown. Turn and cook the other side. Don't have the pan too hot.

Cool on a wire rack while you cook the rest of the batch. Serve with jam and a little dollop of whipped cream or thick yoghurt, and perhaps a little berry or piece of fresh fruit to garnish. Pikelets freeze well but they always seem best freshly made.

Prep time 8 minutes
Cook time 40 minutes per batch

MAKES 20

This is not my own Aunty Peg's recipe but is written in my mum's handwriting, and she is not sure who 'Peg' is, but these are always known as Aunty Peg's Ginger Gems in our family. They are a real winner for an afternoon tea.

AUNTY PEG'S GINGER GEMS

- *50 g butter*
- *2 tablespoons golden syrup*
- *1 egg, at room temperature*
- *½ cup milk, at room temperature*
- *1 teaspoon baking soda*
- *½ cup sugar*
- *1 cup flour*
- *3 teaspoons ground ginger*

Preheat the oven to 200°C. Place the gem irons in the oven to heat up.

Place the butter and golden syrup in a small saucepan and warm gently over medium heat to melt the butter. Mix together.

Beat the egg, milk and baking soda together in a medium to large mixing bowl. Whisk in the butter and golden syrup mixture, then add the sifted dry ingredients and mix until smoothly combined.

Remove the gem irons from the oven and spray with baking spray. Spoon in the batter, filling the moulds to three-quarters full.

Return to the oven and bake for 12–15 minutes until puffed up and deep golden brown. Cool on a wire rack and repeat with the remaining mixture. Make sure you re-spray the warm irons.

When cold, the gems can be split open and filled with whipped cream and dusted with icing sugar. Some people prefer to butter them while still warm from the oven.

Prep time 5 minutes
Cook time 15 minutes per batch

MAKES 24

Gem irons are quite difficult to buy now but are often available on online auction sites or in junk shops or garage sales. Like old-fashioned rotary egg beaters, they are very desirable items and are often snapped up by kitchenware collectors. Give the washed and dried irons a little oily spray or wipe them with oil on a paper towel to protect them from rusting. My mother claims a bit of rust is good for you – though I'm not sure about that!

These, as far as we know, made their debut in 1793 when James Birch first started selling little 'Eccles Pastry Pies' from his small bakery in the town of Eccles. The shop is still there and selling the cakes, albeit that Greater Manchester has sprawled out to include the town in its city boundaries. I've always known these by their other name – Fly Cemeteries.

Eccles Cakes

- 3 SHEETS PUFF PASTRY (THAWED)
- 50 G BUTTER, SOFTENED
- ¼ CUP BROWN SUGAR
- 1 CUP CURRANTS
- ½ CUP MIXED PEEL
- ½ TEASPOON MIXED SPICE
- ½ CUP MILK
- ½ CUP CASTER SUGAR

Preheat the oven to 200°C. Line a baking tray with baking paper.

Using an 8–10 cm cookie cutter or a large cup as a guide, cut out 12 circles of pastry.

Beat the butter and brown sugar together until creamy and well combined. Add the currants, peel and spice and mix well. Place 2 teaspoons of the filling in the centre of each circle of pastry. Brush the edges of the pastry with milk then gather them up over the filling like a little money bag. Pinch the pastry to seal and enclose the filling securely. Press flat to form a 2-cm-thick filled round parcel.

Place on the tray with the join underneath, allowing room on the tray for them to puff up and spread.

Using a small sharp knife, make three diagonal slits in the top of each pastry. Brush with milk and sprinkle with the caster sugar. Bake for 15–20 minutes until the pastry is crisp and golden brown. Cool on a wire rack as the filling is very hot. Best eaten warm. Can be stored for 2–3 days in an airtight container.

Prep time 20 minutes
Cook time 20 minutes

MAKES 12

RED VELVET CUPCAKES

- 100 g butter, softened to room temperature
- ¾ cup sugar
- 2 eggs
- 1 teaspoon vanilla
- 1 teaspoon white vinegar
- 1 teaspoon baking soda
- 150 ml buttermilk
- 2 teaspoons gel red food colouring
- 1 cup self-raising flour
- ¼ cup cocoa

FOR THE CREAM CHEESE FROSTING

- 125 g butter, softened to room temperature
- 300 g cream cheese (traditional, not lite or spreadable), softened
- ½ teaspoon vanilla
- 3 cups icing sugar
- red sprinkles or decorations (optional)

Preheat the oven to 180°C. Line a 12-cup standard muffin tin with paper cases.

Beat the butter and sugar together until pale and fluffy. Beat in the eggs and vanilla.

In a cup, whisk the vinegar and baking soda together, then mix this into the butter mixture. Add the buttermilk and food colouring. Sift the self-raising flour and cocoa together, then add to the mixture, combining well. Divide the mixture between the paper cases. Bake for 20–25 minutes until firm when gently pressed. Transfer to a wire rack and cool completely. Frost when cold.

To make the frosting, beat the softened butter and cream cheese together until well combined. Add the vanilla and beat in the icing sugar until smooth and fluffy. Pipe or spread onto the cooled cupcakes and decorate with sprinkles as desired. These will keep well for 3 days.

Prep time 40 minutes
Cook time 25 minutes

MAKES 12

THESE ARE VERY POPULAR IN THE CAFÉ. THE COLOUR IS PRETTY, BUT THE FLAVOUR IS ESSENTIALLY CHOCOLATE AND LOVELY WITH CREAM CHEESE FROSTING.

If baking is any labour at all, it's a labour of love. A love that gets passed from generation to generation.

A very simple little high tea treat. These also keep very well in an airtight container and make a wonderful packaged up gift. I often make them at Christmas for little presents.

Chocolate Meringue Kisses

- 40 DARK CHOCOLATE BITS (LITTLE CHOCOLATE KISSES OR CHUNKS OF DARK CHOCOLATE ABOUT 5–6 MM SQUARE)
- 3 EGG WHITES, AT ROOM TEMPERATURE
- 1 CUP CASTER SUGAR
- ½ TEASPOON VANILLA

Preheat the oven to 120°C. Line a baking tray with baking paper. Spread the chocolate bits evenly over the prepared tray.

In a medium-sized metal, glass or china bowl (not plastic), use an electric beater to beat the egg whites until stiff. Slowly, a teaspoon at a time, add the caster sugar with the beater going. This takes quite a long time – 5 minutes at least. The egg whites should be thick and glossy. Add the vanilla and beat well. When you rub a little smear of the mixture between your finger and thumb you shouldn't feel any trace of sugar crystals or grittiness.

Spoon the mixture into a piping bag fitted with a small star nozzle. Pipe a small star of mixture over the top of each chocolate bit. Bake for 35–45 minutes until crispy and dry and the little meringues easily lift off the baking paper. Cool on a wire rack and store in an airtight container for up to 3 weeks.

Variations of these can be made using different fillings, for example macadamia or hazelnuts, broken pieces of candy cane, chocolate raisins, gummy bears or crystallised ginger etc., and different food colourings to colour the meringues.

Prep time 10 minutes
Cook time 45 minutes

MAKES 40

MINI CHRISTMAS MINCE PIES

CHRISTMAS MINCEMEAT
(THIS MAKES ENOUGH FOR 3–4 BATCHES OF MINI MINCE PIES)

- 1 cup raisins
- 1 cup sultanas
- ¾ cup currants
- ¾ cup dried cranberries
- 1 x 150 g packet mixed peel
- ½ cup red glacé cherries, cut in half
- ½ cup green glacé cherries, cut in half
- 1 cup brown sugar
- grated rind of 1 lemon
- grated rind of 1 orange
- 3 teaspoons mixed spice
- ¼ cup brandy, rum, or orange liqueur (I use Cointreau)

Place all the ingredients in a food processor and mix to a pulpy combined consistency. Place in a clean screwtop jar and refrigerate. Can be kept for up to a year. Periodically turn the jar upside down then right way up to keep the liquid moving in the fruit, keeping it nice and moist.

PASTRY

- 125 g cold butter, cut into small pieces
- 1 cup flour
- ½ cup icing sugar

Preheat the oven to 180°C. Spray a 12-cup mini-muffin tray with baking spray.

Place the butter in a food processor. Add the flour and icing sugar and run the machine until the mixture clumps together around the blade. Roll into a sausage shape and cut into 16 equal pieces. Press 12 of these into the bases and up the sides of the sprayed muffin cups. I use a tart tamper for this. Chill the pastry-lined mini-muffin tray in the freezer for 10 minutes. This is an important step as the pastry should be cold when going into the oven.

Using a small teaspoon, fill each cup three-quarters full of Christmas mincemeat. Return to the freezer.

Squeeze the remaining 4 balls of pastry together. Place on a lightly floured board or bench and roll out. Cut out 12 little stars. Press these onto the tops of the chilled pies, then immediately place in the oven. Bake for 12–15 minutes until golden brown. Leave in the tins for 5 minutes until they are cool enough to handle. Carefully twist in the tins to free the bases, then use the tip of a little paring knife to ease out of the tins to cool on a wire rack. Dust with icing sugar to serve.

These will keep in an airtight container for a week and can be frozen.

Prep time 30 minutes
Cook time 15 minutes

MAKES 12 BITE-SIZE PIES

WHY WAIT UNTIL CHRISTMAS?
THESE ARE TOO GOOD TO ONLY
EAT ONCE A YEAR.

THIS IS MY GRANNY WIN'S RECIPE AND IT WORKS A TREAT. A FEW LITTLE TIPS THAT HELP WITH SUCCESS HAVE BEEN INCLUDED.

Chocolate Éclairs

- 100 G BUTTER
- 300 ML HOT WATER
- 1 CUP FLOUR
- 4 EGGS

Preheat the oven to 200°C. Spray a tray with baking spray and line with baking paper. Run the paper-lined tray under cold water and shake off the excess water. This provides a little moisture to steam and help puff up the éclairs. You can use a silicone sheet on the tray in place of the baking paper.

Place the butter and water in a medium-sized saucepan and bring to the boil, melting the butter. As soon as it is boiling, remove from the heat. Add the flour all at once and beat with a wooden spoon or spatula until it comes together in a clump, pulling cleanly away from the sides of the pan. Place the mixture in a large bowl and cool for a few minutes until just warm. This is important as it will overcook the eggs if too hot. When cooled, beat in the eggs one at a time, mixing in well before adding the next egg. I use the paddle blade attachment on my electric mixer for this job.

The mixture will be shiny and quite glossy. Spoon into a large piping bag fitted with a plain 1 cm nozzle. Pipe out sausages of mixture about 7 cm long onto the prepared tray. Leave plenty of room around each one as they puff up in the oven. Cook for 10 minutes then turn the oven down to 170°C and cook for a further 25 minutes until golden, puffed and crispy on the outside.

Don't be tempted to open the oven door as they cook.

An oven thermometer is handy to check the oven's exact temperature and I always use the fan-bake function for even cooking.

When you remove the éclairs from the oven they should be shiny and golden brown. As soon as they have cooled enough to handle, slice them open with a small, sharp serrated knife to let the steam out. If you need to, any uncooked éclair mixture can be scraped out of the insides and you may pop them back in the oven for 3–4 minutes to completely dry the insides out. Cool on a wire rack.

Ice with chocolate icing (see page 130) and fill with sweetened whipped cream or patisserie cream 2–3 hours before eating. Any longer and they may go soggy (which is actually my favourite way to have them, as leftovers in the morning!).

The éclair cases can be made a few days in advance and kept unfilled in an airtight container. I usually refresh them with a few minutes in a warm oven to re-crisp.

Prep time 10 minutes
Cook time 35 minutes

MAKES APPROX 20

Macarons have become very popular in the last few years, with special little macaron shops popping up all over town. I love these fashionable little delicacies but they can be a bit temperamental to master. I have included all my tips and hints (see page 277) to help you get them perfect every time. You get a lot of brownie points being good at macarons so it is worth persevering with them.

MACARONS

- 1 cup ground almonds
- 1¼ cups icing sugar
- 3 egg whites (100 g)
- pinch of salt
- ⅓ cup caster sugar

Line 2 baking trays with baking paper. Lightly spray the paper with baking spray, then wipe any excess spray off with a paper towel.

Place the ground almonds and icing sugar in a food processor. Whiz until very fine. Sieve to discard any bits so that the almond mixture is uniformly smooth and fine.

Place the egg whites and salt in a small metal, glass or china bowl (not plastic). Using an electric mixer, beat until small peaks form. Slowly add the caster sugar, beating on high speed, until the mixture becomes smooth and glossy and firm peaks form.

Add half the almond mixture to the eggs and fold in carefully. Add the other half and fold in until the mixture is smooth and glossy.

Spoon the mixture into a piping bag with a 1.5 cm plain piping nozzle. Pipe onto the prepared trays with 4–5 cm between them.

Tap the trays a couple of times on the bench to 'settle' the mixture and remove any little air bubbles.

With a wet finger, dab down any peaks so that the surface is flattened and smooth. Allow to rest and dry slightly for 40–50 minutes before baking. They will form a kind of flat skin on the surface. This is an important step, so don't be impatient to get them into the oven.

Preheat the oven to 130°C.

Bake for 20–30 minutes. Allow to cool on the tray, then carefully peel them off the paper before filling with your favourite filling. See overleaf for flavour variations.

These keep well, unfilled, in an airtight container for up to a week. When filled, they keep for a couple of days in an airtight container. Can be frozen.

Prep time 20 minutes
Rest time 50 minutes
Cook time 30 minutes

MAKES ABOUT 18–20 SANDWICHED-TOGETHER

MACARONS – CONTINUED

Macaron Variations

COFFEE
Add 1 tablespoon of instant coffee powder to the mixture. These are lovely with chocolate ganache filling (see page 293).

MIXED SPICE
Add 2 teaspoons of mixed spice to the mixture. These are lovely with a chocolate ganache filling (see page 293).

ORANGE OR LEMON
Add yellow or orange food colouring to the mixture and fill with lemon-coloured or flavoured butter cream or fill with lemon curd (see page 293) – very yummy!

ROSEWATER
Add ½–1 teaspoon rosewater plus some pink food colouring to the mixture. These are lovely with a rosewater butter cream filling (see page 209).

RASPBERRY OR STRAWBERRY
Add some pink food colouring to the mixture and fill with raspberry- or strawberry-flavoured butter cream (see page 290) or thick fruit jam.

PISTACHIO
Use ½ cup of ground almonds and ½ cup of ground pistachios in the mixture and a drop or two of green food colouring. Add ¼ cup ground or finely chopped pistachios to green butter cream.

CHOCOLATE
Add 1 tablespoon of dark Dutch cocoa to the mix. Fill with chocolate ganache (see page 293) or chocolate butter cream (see page 290).

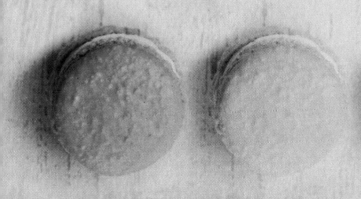

Macaron Tips & Tricks

- USING A FOOD PROCESSOR TO MIX THE GROUND ALMONDS AND ICING SUGAR IS IMPORTANT AS THIS ENSURES THE FINENESS OF THE MIXTURE, AND THE RESULT IS THE TOPS OF THE MACARONS ARE SMOOTH AND SHINY.

- EGG WHITES – THESE COME IN ALL SIZES, SO IF THEY LOOK BIGGER OR SMALLER THEN YOU NEED TO WEIGH THEM. THE 3 EGG WHITES IN THIS MIXTURE SHOULD BE ABOUT 100 G.

- THE MIXTURE SHOULD BE THE CORRECT CONSISTENCY – NOT TOO THICK OR TOO RUNNY. IF THIN, IT MAY BE BECAUSE OF INITIALLY UNDER-WHISKING THE EGG WHITES OR ADDING TOO MUCH LIQUID COLOURING.

- PREPARING TRAYS – ALWAYS LINE THE TRAYS AND LIGHTLY GREASE WITH BAKING SPRAY. MACARONS DO LIKE TO STICK! I SPRAY THE PAPER THEN WIPE OFF EXCESS SPRAY WITH A PAPER TOWEL.

- TRY TO KEEP PIPING AS EVEN AS POSSIBLE. KEEP THE PIPED MIXTURE QUITE FLAT, AS ROUNDER ONES TEND TO OOZE AND SPREAD.

- A WET FINGER WORKS WELL TO REMOVE PEAKS OR POINTS. THE ADDED MOISTURE FROM YOUR FINGER WILL MEAN THEY MAY NEED A LITTLE LONGER TO DRY OUT BEFORE BAKING.

- HAVING A PIECE OF BAKING PAPER WITH CIRCLES DRAWN ON IT IN FELT PEN TO USE AS A GUIDE IS HANDY FOR UNIFORM SIZING. I KEEP THIS STENCILLED SHEET ON A CARDBOARD PAPER TOWEL ROLL IN MY BAKING CUPBOARD. YOU LAY IT UNDER YOUR SHEET OF BAKING PAPER TO USE AS A TRACKING GUIDE WHEN PIPING THE MACARONS OUT.

I get a kick out of friends
demanding seconds.

If you love the hit of coffee then these will totally satisfy your craving, and are obviously the perfect accompaniment to a cup of coffee. This recipe uses Bushells Coffee & Chicory Essence, which can be found in the coffee section of New Zealand supermarkets. You can substitute 2 tablespoons of instant coffee dissolved in 2 tablespoons of boiling water, but the coffee & chicory essence is the best flavour.

Coffee Lovers' Baby Cakes

- 150 G BUTTER, SOFTENED
- ¾ CUP CASTER SUGAR
- 3 EGGS
- 2 TABLESPOONS COFFEE & CHICORY ESSENCE
- 1 CUP SELF-RAISING FLOUR

For the icing
- 150 G BUTTER, SOFTENED
- 2 CUPS ICING SUGAR
- 2 TABLESPOONS COFFEE & CHICORY ESSENCE
- 50 G DARK CHOCOLATE TO GARNISH, MELTED

Preheat the oven to 170°C. Line a standard muffin tray with paper cases.

Beat the butter and caster sugar together until pale and fluffy. Add the eggs and essence, then mix in the flour. Spoon the mixture into the paper cases. Bake for 15–18 minutes, until firm when gently pressed in the middle. Cool on a wire rack.

Remove from cases when cold and split in half with a serrated knife.

To make the icing, beat the butter and icing sugar together until well combined. Add the essence and mix well. Sandwich the tops and bottoms of each cake together with icing and pipe each top decoratively. Using a potato peeler, slice curls of chocolate to garnish each little cake.

Prep time 15 minutes
Cook time 18 minutes

MAKES 18
CUPCAKE-SIZED CAKES

This is my all-time most popular recipe. People from all over the country have told me that this is their party special. I've been making them for over 40 years. The original recipe came from North Carolina but I have adapted it so much and made quite a few changes so that it is hardly recognisable now. They are always a hit and I think best served slightly warmed.

JO'S SPECIAL MINI PECAN PIES

FOR THE PASTRY
- 125 g butter
- 1 cup flour
- ½ cup icing sugar

FOR THE FILLING
- 1 cup pecan nuts
- 60 g butter, melted
- 1 egg
- 1 cup brown sugar
- 1 teaspoon vanilla

Spray 16 mini-muffin cups with baking spray.

Place the pastry ingredients in a food processor and run the machine until the pastry clumps around the blade. Divide the pastry into 16 small balls and, with floured hands, press into the bases and up the sides of 16 mini-muffin cups. Using a tart tamper makes this job easy and ensures the pastry sides are an even thickness.

Place the pastry-lined tins in the freezer to chill for 30 minutes until the pastry is really firm and hard.

Preheat the oven to 180°C.

Divide the nuts between the pastry-lined cups, breaking the nuts in half if necessary.

Whisk the melted butter, egg, brown sugar and vanilla until smooth, but somewhat gluey. Using a small jug, pour approximately a teaspoon of this mixture into each nut-filled cup and bake for 20–25 minutes until the pastry is golden brown and the filling set and crisp.

You will not use all this mixture. There is enough for two batches. It is hard to halve an egg, so in fact you have a double-batch of this filling. To use it all just double the quantity of pastry.

Remove from the oven and cool for 5 minutes in the tins until the pies are cool enough to handle. Give each pie a little twist to loosen the bottom, then carefully lift out with the tip of a small paring knife to cool completely on a wire rack.

These are delicious served warm as a dessert. Can be stored in an airtight container for up to 2 weeks. They also freeze very well.

Prep time 15 minutes
Chill time 30 minutes
Cook time 25 minutes

MAKES 16

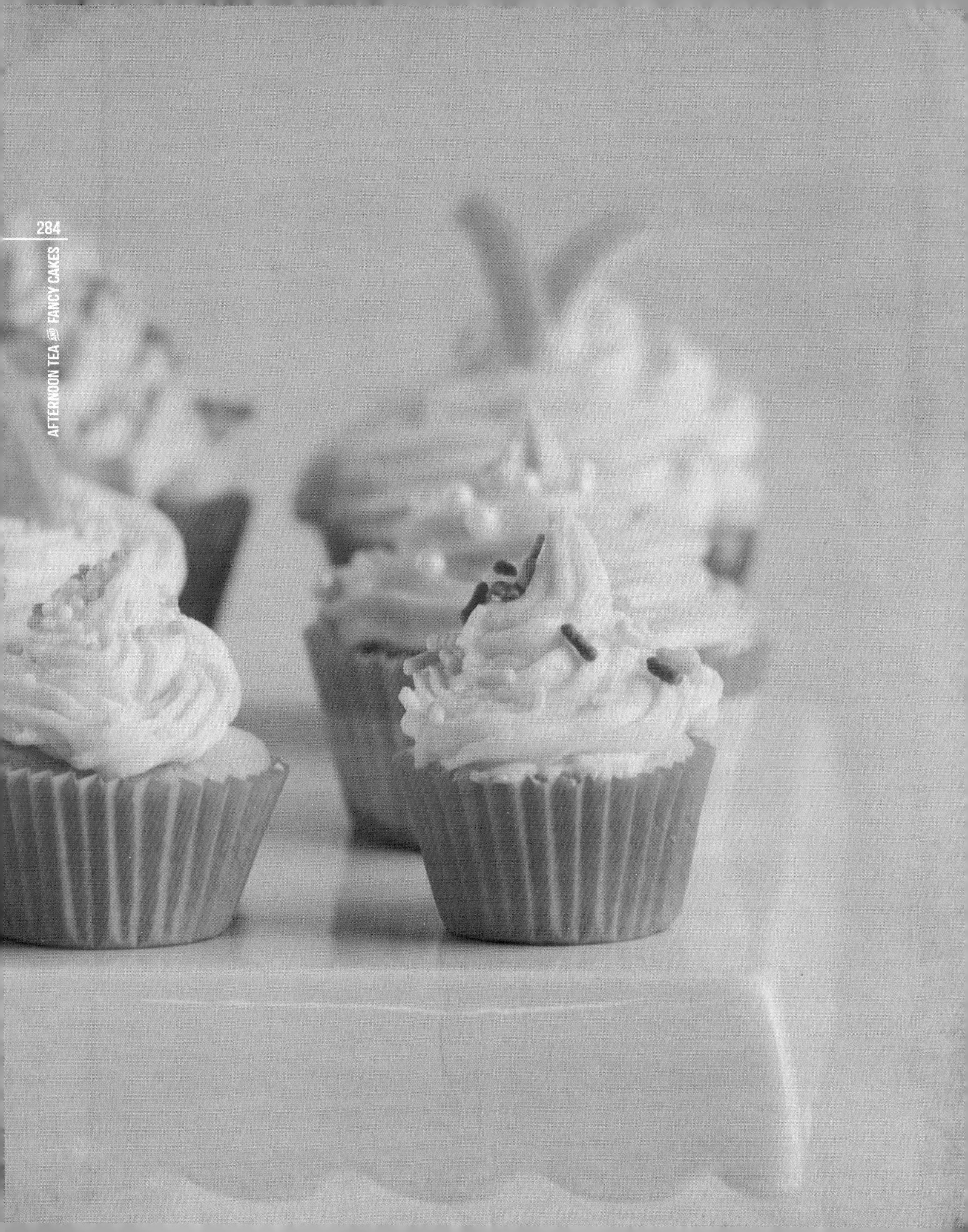

A good basic cupcake recipe that makes a moist, delicious little base so you can be ultra-creative with the decorating. I use vanilla butter frosting piped in nice swirly patterns.

Vanilla Cupcakes

- 125 G BUTTER
- ¾ CUP CASTER SUGAR
- 1 TEASPOON VANILLA
- 2 EGGS
- 1½ CUPS SELF-RAISING FLOUR
- ½ TEASPOON BAKING POWDER
- 1 TABLESPOON SOUR CREAM
- ½ CUP MILK

Preheat the oven to 180°C. Line a 12-cup muffin tin with paper cases and lightly spray with baking spray.

Beat the butter, sugar and vanilla together until pale and creamy. Add the eggs, one at a time, beating well after each addition. Stir in the flour, baking powder, sour cream and milk and mix until smooth.

Place spoonfuls of mixture into the prepared cases. Bake for 15 minutes.

Allow to cool and then ice with vanilla butter frosting.

Prep time 10 minutes plus decorating
Cook time 15 minutes

 **MAKES 12**

Vanilla Butter Frosting

- 250 G BUTTER, SOFTENED
- 2 CUPS ICING SUGAR, SIFTED
- 1–2 TABLESPOONS BOILING WATER
- 1 TEASPOON VANILLA
- FOOD COLOURING AS REQUIRED

Beat the butter until light and creamy. Gradually add the icing sugar and boiling water. Add the vanilla and colour if required. The frosting should be a fluffy consistency. Extra icing sugar may be required to produce this texture. Pipe onto the cooled cupcakes.

These have masses of variations: by using different essences, i.e. coffee, strawberry or coconut; by using different frosting colours and flavours, or any number of sprinkles and sweets to decorate.

They are best eaten in 2 days but will freeze really well un-iced.

Lamingtons are always popular treats, perhaps more so in Australia where they feature big-time in the foodie culture. I prefer the strawberry 'pink' lamingtons, but others favour the chocolate ones. Big plates of each variety get pretty much equal patronage in the café.

They are quite easy although a bit messy to make, and of course you can purchase a supermarket slab of sponge cake to make the whole process quicker. We always make our own sponge the day before for best results.

CAFÉ STYLE LAMINGTONS

FOR THE SPONGE CAKE

- *4 eggs*
- *pinch of salt*
- *1 cup caster sugar*
- *1¼ cups flour*
- *1½ teaspoons baking powder*
- *75 g butter, melted*

Preheat the oven to 190°C. Spray a 20–21 cm square cake tin with baking spray and line with baking paper.

Beat the eggs, salt and caster sugar together until pale and thick. Fold in the sifted flour and baking powder and the melted butter. Mix until well combined. Pour into the prepared tin and bake for 30–35 minutes until the centre springs back when gently pressed and the colour is golden brown.

Leave to cool in the tin for 10 minutes then carefully turn out to cool completely on a wire rack.

When cold, wrap in tinfoil or cling film and keep until the next day. When ready to assemble the lamingtons, use a serrated knife to cut the sponge into 4–5 cm squares. (I find freezing the sponge for half an hour is helpful to make nice clean cut surfaces without too many crumbs.)

STRAWBERRY LAMINGTONS

- *1 packet strawberry (or raspberry) jelly crystals*
- *1 cup boiling water*
- *½ cup cold water*
- *2 cups coconut, to coat the lamingtons*
- *cream & jam or strawberries, to serve*

Mix the jelly crystals with the boiling water and stir to dissolve. Add the cold water and chill in the fridge until the jelly is gluggy and beginning to set – about 30–45 minutes. It should be the thickness of egg whites.

Spread the coconut in a shallow tray. Dip the sponge squares into the jelly then dip into or sprinkle generously with the coconut, shaking off the excess. Place on a wire rack to dry and set.

When set, make a slit in the lamingtons and fill with whipped cream and top with a dollop of jam or a strawberry slice to garnish.

CHOCOLATE LAMINGTONS

- 2 tablespoons cocoa
- 25 g butter, melted
- 6 tablespoons boiling water
- 2¼ cups icing sugar
- 2 cups coconut
- cream, to serve

Sift the cocoa into a bowl, then add the melted butter and boiling water and mix together. Mix in the icing sugar to make a runny chocolate icing.

Spread the coconut in a shallow tray. Dip the sponge squares into the chocolate, then dip into or sprinkle generously with the coconut, shaking off the excess. Place on a wire rack to dry and set.

When set, make a slit in the lamingtons and fill with whipped cream.

Lamingtons will keep in an airtight container for a couple of days but they are best eaten freshly made. The sponge cake freezes well if wrapped in cling film or placed in a plastic container in the freezer.

Prep time 10 minutes plus 15 minutes assembly
Cook time 35 minutes

MAKES 16

A delicate little passionfruit cream-filled puff is the perfect high tea treat. Some people like to drizzle them with passionfruit icing as well, but we always just dust with a light snowing of icing sugar.

For the passionfruit icing

- 2–2½ CUPS ICING SUGAR, SIFTED
- 3 TABLESPOONS PASSIONFRUIT PULP

Mix the icing sugar and passionfruit pulp together until a smooth icing consistency forms that you can pour and dribble down the sides of the puffs.

Passionfruit Cream Puffs

- 100 G BUTTER
- 300 ML HOT WATER
- 1 CUP FLOUR
- 4 EGGS

Preheat the oven to 200°C. Spray a tray with baking spray and line with baking paper. Run the paper-lined tray under cold water and shake off the excess water. This will provide a little steam and help puff up the choux pastry. You can also use a silicone sheet on the tray in place of the baking paper.

Place the butter and water in a medium-sized saucepan and bring to the boil, melting the butter. As soon as it is boiling, remove from the heat. Add the flour all at once and beat with a wooden spoon or spatula until it comes together in a clump, pulling cleanly away from the sides of the pan. Place the mixture in a large bowl and cool for a few minutes until just warm. This is important, as it will overcook the eggs if too hot. When cooled, beat in the eggs, one at a time, mixing in well before adding the next egg. I use the paddle blade attachment on my electric mixer for this job.

The mixture will be shiny and quite glossy. Spoon into a large piping bag fitted with a plain 1 cm nozzle. Pipe out little balls of mixture about 3–4 cm in diameter onto the prepared tray. Leave plenty of room around each one as they puff up in the oven. Cook for 10 minutes, then turn the oven down to 170°C and cook for a further 15–20 minutes until golden, puffed and crispy on the outside. Don't be tempted to open the oven door while they are cooking.

An oven thermometer is handy to check the oven's exact temperature, and I always use the fan-bake function for even cooking.

When you remove the puffs from the oven they should be shiny and golden brown. As soon as they have cooled enough to handle, slice open with a small, sharp serrated knife to let the steam out. If you need to, any uncooked puff mixture can be scraped out of the insides and you can pop the puffs back in the oven for 3–4 minutes to completely dry the insides out. Cool on a wire rack.

Prep time 10 minutes
Cook time 30 minutes

MAKES 25–28

For the passionfruit cream filling

- ½ CUP PASSIONFRUIT PULP, INCLUDING SEEDS
- ¼ CUP ICING SUGAR, SIFTED
- 300 ML CREAM, WHIPPED TO FIRM PEAKS

Fold the passionfruit pulp and icing sugar into the whipped cream.

When the puffs are cold, fill with passionfruit cream and replace the lids.

To serve, either pour over the passionfruit icing, allowing it to drip down the sides of the puffs, or alternatively, dust with icing sugar. Allow to set then stack on a plate to serve.

ICINGS, FROSTINGS AND ACCOMPANIMENTS

BUTTER CREAM FROSTING

- 100 g butter, at room temperature
- ½ teaspoon vanilla
- 2–2½ cups icing sugar, sifted if lumpy

Beat the butter and vanilla together until soft, light and fluffy. Gradually beat in the icing sugar to a desired smooth, spreadable consistency. A few drops of boiling water may be needed to get the right consistency.

For Chocolate Butter Cream Frosting

Add 1–2 tablespoons of cocoa to the basic butter cream mixture.

For Flavoured Butter Cream

Add a few drops of food colouring and flavouring to the basic recipe. For example:
– peppermint essence with green food colouring
– raspberry or strawberry essence with pink food colouring
– sweetened coffee and chicory essence for coffee-flavoured butter cream.

BRANDY BUTTER FROSTING

- 200 g butter, at room temperature
- 2½–3 cups icing sugar, sifted if lumpy
- ¼ cup brandy

Beat all the ingredients together in a food processor until smooth and fluffy.

BUTTER ICING

- 25 g butter, melted
- 2–2½ cups icing sugar, sifted if lumpy
- 1–2 tablespoons boiling water

Beat all the ingredients together, adding enough icing sugar to get to the required spreadable consistency. For runny icings that need to drip down the sides of cakes you will need more water but for firmer ones to ice biscuits add less water.

For Flavoured Butter Icing

– for chocolate, add 2–3 tablespoons cocoa
– for vanilla, add ½ teaspoon vanilla
– for orange, add 1 teaspoon grated orange rind
– for rose, add 1–2 teaspoons rosewater

FRESH LEMON ICING

My favourite icing for Banana Cake.

- grated rind & juice of 1 lemon
- 25 g butter, melted
- 2½–3 cups icing sugar, sifted if lumpy

Mix all the ingredients together, beating to ensure a smooth consistency. Add as much icing sugar as required to get the right consistency depending on whether you intend to drizzle over the cake to run down the sides or have a firmer, spreadable icing.

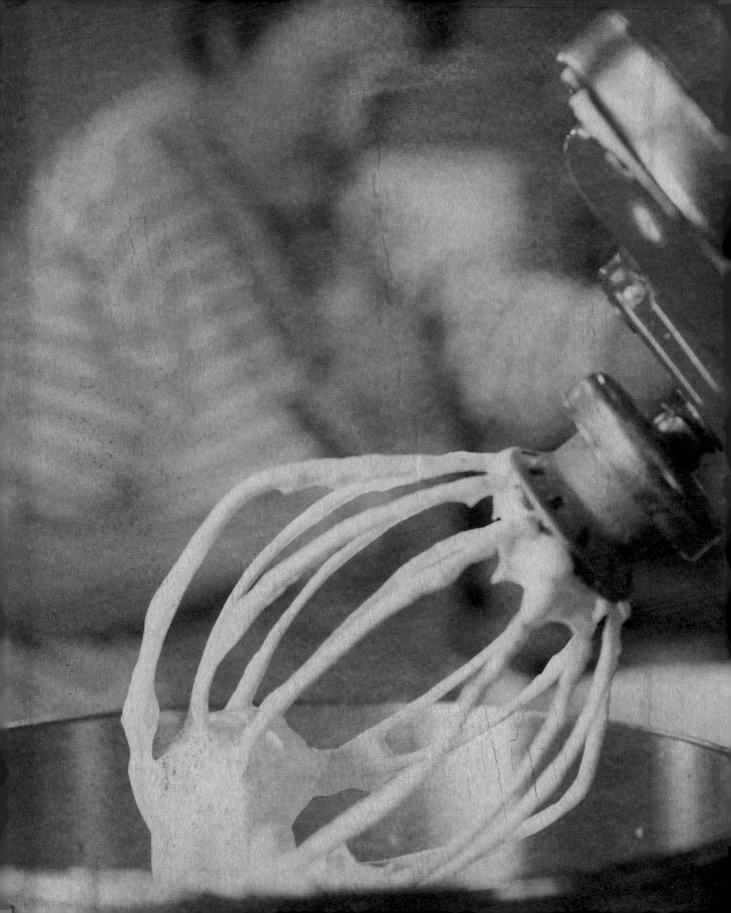

CARAMEL ICING

- 1 cup brown sugar
- 25 g butter
- 2 tablespoons full-fat milk
- 1–1½ cups icing sugar, sifted if lumpy

Place the brown sugar, butter and milk in a small saucepan over medium heat. Stir until the butter is melted and the sugar dissolved. Beat in enough icing sugar to reach the desired consistency. A few extra drops of milk may be required to achieve the right consistency for spreading.

CREAM CHEESE FROSTING

Softened or spreadable cream cheese contains too much water so I use traditional or regular cream cheese when making this frosting.

- 125 g cream cheese, at room temperature
- 50 g butter, at room temperature
- 2½–3 cups icing sugar
- ½ teaspoon vanilla

Beat all the ingredients together until light and fluffy and the desired smooth frosting consistency.

CHOCOLATE GANACHE

- 400 g chopped dark chocolate (50–60% cocoa solids will be sufficient here)
- 150 ml milk
- 200 ml cream

Place all the ingredients in a medium-sized saucepan and stir over gentle heat as the mixture comes up to the boil. Stir as it gently boils, making sure the chocolate is melted and the mixture is smooth. Cool to room temperature, about 2 hours.

LEMON CURD

Makes about 2½ cups.

- 4 large, juicy lemons
- 4 eggs, beaten (or 8 egg yokes)
- 2 cups sugar
- 200 g butter, cubed

Wash the lemons then finely grate the rind and squeeze the juice into a small saucepan. Add the beaten eggs, sugar and butter cubes. Constantly stir with a wire whisk over very gentle heat until the sugar dissolves and the mixture thickens. Keep the heat very low and don't be tempted to speed it up or to stop stirring as it thickens.

Cool, then pour into a plastic container and store in the fridge. Keeps for 2–3 weeks refrigerated.

Acknowledgements

My special thanks to my fabulous photographer and friend Jae Frew. Jae has done much more than just the photography for this book – he has been the designer and produced the whole lovely 'look' of the book. Thank you, Jae.

To Susan Elijas for fabulous styling and design work. Jo Patterson, Jane Rangiwahia, Claudia Frew and Victoria Madison for lots of baking, recipe testing and food styling. Petrina Jose for help with design and layout. The staff at Seagars of Oxford, especially Leanne Wheeler and Trish Craig for all the coffees and hard work behind the scenes. Maree O'Neill for getting me scrubbed and zhuzhed up for the photography. Ross, for your typing and (sometimes) helpful advice and support.

Jenny Hellen and her team at Random House. Thank you for your continuing support and encouragement.

Dawn and Richard Sparks for the loan of your wonderful collection of vintage kitchen paraphernalia – your museum in Rangiora is a treasure house. To my Italian kids, Federica Contardi and Davide Zerilli, your assistance with styling and photography was such an inspiration and help.

And to my very dear mother, Fay Wellwood, who always helps me with her fun kitchen reminiscing and stories, and researching the old handwritten books handed down from the women in my family who have baked before us.

Granny Win (third from left) — Butterscotch Date Fingers, page 89

Emily Cross — Emily's Lemon Shortcake, page 110

Claudia Frew — Claudia's Rosewater Cake, page 209

Granny Fay — My darling mother, Fay, famous in our family for Fay's Mumbles, page 133 (and cheekily known as Fanny Gray by her grand- and great-grandchildren)

Aunt Annie — Aunt Annie's Louise Cake, page 113

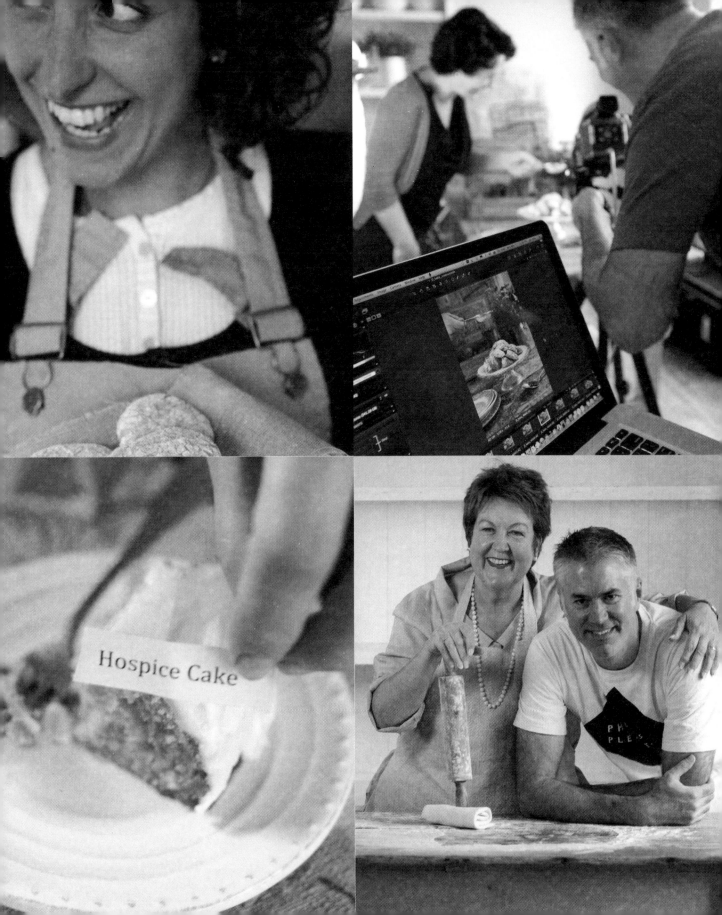

Hospice Cake

INDEX